Communism and China: Ideology in Flux

Communism and China

Ideology in Flux

Benjamin I. Schwartz

Harvard University Press : Cambridge, Massachusetts

CONTENTS

Communism and China: Ideology in Flux

ABBREVIATIONS

CCP:	Chinese Communist Party
CPSU:	Communist Party of the Soviet Union
FLN:	Fédération de Liberation Nationale
JPRS:	Joint Publications Research Service
N.E.P.:	New Economic Policy
PLA:	People's Liberation Army
WFTU:	World Federation of Trade Unions

COMMUNISM AND CHINA:
IDEOLOGY IN FLUX

The study of contemporary affairs has become a highly respectable—even a dominant—pursuit of the American academy. One is indeed astonished by the charge of young adherents of the New Left that what is being taught at the universities is irrelevant to the burning issues of the day. In fact, an enormous proportion of the energies and resources of the academic world are now devoted to the production of experts on the "problems of the day." To be sure, what the new radicals reject essentially is not the present orientation of social studies, which is overwhelmingly contemporary, but the whole pathos of "scientific expertise." They have revolted in favor of moral passion and immediate involvement. The more political-minded among them have hardly revolted against an orientation to the actual which is already fully entrenched.

What I should like to consider briefly are not the attacks of the new radicalism but the objections from another quarter not now powerfully represented on the American academic scene. In this view, all efforts to grasp the inner meaning of the passing events of the day can be nothing but high-order journalism at best. The documentation is highly incomplete and defective. Our passions, biases, and anxieties are immediately involved and there is considerable room for suspicion that all our analyses are "policy-oriented." Furthermore, the mixture of "high theory" and news analysis often produces unfortunate results for both. Narrowly conceived, rigid "models" and "conceptual schemes" are forced onto the rich, chaotic, and infinitely varied flow of events, constricting the imagination and leaving the mind unprepared for unforeseen possibilities and combinations. Or conversely, new models and "empirical hypotheses" claiming general and enduring validity are hastily constructed on the shifting sands of evanescent and quite particular conjunctures of circumstances. There is the added threat of the impoverishment of the human intellect and spirit which can result from the imposition of narrowly constrictive canons of relevance whether by middle-aged social scientists or young new radicals. However agonizing and obsessive the social and political crises of the moment may be for all of us, the attempt to orient the whole intellectual life of the university about these crises may insure the irrelevance of all of our present ideas to those who follow us. There is nothing quite so irrelevant as yesterday's crisis and yesterday's news analysis.

There are obvious retorts which can be made to this kind of attack on the academic study of current affairs. If the documentation of the emerging scene is defective, there are built-in limitations in all types of historical documentation even though the "whole story is in." While the historian's passions and anxieties may not be as immediately engaged as those of the student of contemporary affairs, while he may enjoy a certain distance from his subject, in the end he does not escape his own philosophic assumptions and present concerns even when writing about ancient Egypt. All history, as has been well stated, is in some sense the history of the present. One may go on to stress the positive superiorities of contemporary studies. It is precisely because they may affect the course of future policy, precisely because they deal with the "existing" problems of the "real world" that current studies hold the promise of new insights.

While all the writings gathered in this volume are definitely concerned with the "emerging present," I shall not here launch a fanatical defense of the respectability of the study of current affairs in academic institutions. In mid-century America this hardly seems necessary. It is rather the possible human relevance of ancient Egypt which requires defense against the advocates of both the new technocracy and the new radicalism. Indeed, one feels a strong need to disassociate oneself from some of the more strident claims of the partisans of the contemporary. Some of them are firmly convinced that their social science "methodologies" have immunized them against passion, bias, and identification with interests. It is my own conviction that whatever insights are achieved in the study of contemporary affairs are achieved in the full presence of all our passions, anxieties, and particular commitments. These cannot be exorcized. Others—on the new left—are firmly convinced that their own righteousness guarantees the validity of their ideas; and some have convinced themselves that nothing "pre-modern" can possibly be relevant to the situation of modern man. It is my conviction that we can have no preconceived idea of what areas of human experience—modern or pre-modern—may be relevant to the human situation.

I would urge that the *ultimate* justification of the study of contemporary affairs at the university is not very different from the justification of historic studies. Such studies involve vital intellectual issues—vital not only to the solution of current issues but to larger, more durable concerns. They have their own limitations and drawbacks, but so do all empirical investigations. Presumably the difference between the intellectually serious and the typical journalistic approach to contemporary affairs is that the average journalist is quite convinced that he is a practical man dealing

3

with the "hard facts," while he is often blissfully unaware of his own implicit and explicit assumptions; but the student of contemporary affairs should be acutely aware that he cannot for a moment deal with the world around him without bringing into play and putting to the test all his implicit and explicit political, social, and even philosophic assumptions. It is indeed precisely this relevance to the larger, more enduring intellectual issues that ultimately justifies the study of the emerging present within the walls of the academy.

The study of contemporary China is, of course, peculiarly vulnerable to all the attacks of traditional scholarship. The documentation is woefully incomplete and problematic. Our emotions and interests are immediately involved and we cannot help but be concerned with policy. I would, nevertheless, contend that the academic study of contemporary China is ultimately justified, not by its topicality, not by the fact that it is an important issue of the day, but by its relevance to a whole range of significant human issues for which it opens rich new areas of inquiry. The assumption is that if all the conflicts between Washington and Peking were to be resolved tomorrow, the study of contemporary China would not cease to be of absorbing intellectual interest. It is a study which relates itself to an infinite variety of questions. How do ideas relate to political, economic, and social behavior? What is nationalism, and how does it relate to ideologies with transnational claims? What happens when a body of ideas emerges in one culture and in one set of historic circumstances and then becomes a ruling orthodoxy in a society arising out of a different culture and involved in a different set of historic circumstances? What is the relationship between culture and modernization? What is modernization? And, on a somewhat more concrete level, what is Communism

4

(Marxist-Leninist Communism) and whither is it moving? Where is Chinese society moving?

In the following pages, I have gathered together a selection of pieces written over a span of some thirteen years in an effort to wrestle with aspects of the protean evolution of Communist China both in terms of its relations to "world Communism" and in terms of its internal developments. It is not my concern to defend every opinion or every formulation expressed in these pieces, nor have I attempted to rewrite them in terms of later hindsights. My main object here is to reconsider and restate some of the assumptions and concerns which underlay them. They were not written to confirm any explicit, preestablished "methodology." Yet in reexamining them, I am aware of certain pervasive implicit concerns and assumptions which I remain, on the whole, prepared to defend. They by no means deal with every order of question which might be raised concerning the evolution of contemporary China or of Communism, and some might even question whether the essays deal with what they consider to be the questions of paramount importance. The first order of business must therefore be a vindication of the significance of the questions examined in these writings.

Most of them concern the ideas, attitudes, and policies of the leading "decision-making" individuals and groups in Peking and in what has been known as the Communist world. They do not attempt to deal *directly* with the grass roots—with the lives of most of the seven hundred million inhabitants of China—and hence might even be thought to reflect a lack of concern for the masses. On the other hand, some think that in focusing on the ideas, policies, and decisions of a leading group, one is ignoring the "underlying" impersonal forces and laws of history of which the leaders are presumably the mere instruments. In both

5

of these views, incidentally, the ideas and policies of the leaders are treated as being either infinitely more than the conscious responses of determinate individuals or else as completely irrelevant. To many adherents of Maoism, Mao is the embodiment of the World Historic Forces, hence it is both wrong and irreverent to treat his ideas as the reactions of a given empirical individual to the situations which confront him. On the other hand, to many who speak in terms of such categories as "The Process of Modernization," "Political Modernization," "The Chinese Revolutionary Process," "Political Culture," and other doctrines concerning the presumed laws of sociopolitical development, what the leaders say may be completely irrelevant to the course of their behavior, which is obviously determined by forces completely beyond their control and probably outside the range of their consciousness.

It is quite true that none of these pieces are directly concerned with the lives of the masses. In part, this is due to the nature of the documentation on which we have been forced to rely. This material is *mainly* relevant to the policies and responses of the leadership. To the extent that new material such as interview data and travel reports do throw light on what is happening in China at the grass-roots levels, such data is exceedingly welcome, and every honest effort to investigate and reconstruct life at the grass roots, however difficult and problematic the data may be, is certainly welcome. Nevertheless, the concern with the ideas, policies, and attitudes of the leadership needs no justification. We are dealing with a situation in which small elites and even individuals are in a position to make decisions that profoundly affect the lives of the masses. This by no means implies the omnipotence of these elites. On the contrary, one of our persistent themes is the degree to which the ideas and policies of the leaders are frustrated and modified by the imperatives created by unforeseen circumstances. Among these circumstances are the reactions overt and covert of vast masses of people to the policies of the leadership. The reaction of Chinese peasants to the "Great Leap Forward" policies was an essential factor in the subsequent fate of those policies. In the long run one need not doubt that the silent attitudes and life circumstances of the inhabitants of China's countless villages will have as much to do with shaping China's future political and cultural development as Mao's visions or the policies of his confreres and opponents. Nevertheless, in the period of the emerging present considered in this volume, the ideas and goals of the leadership remain a variable of decisive importance. Furthermore, being unable to accept the belief that all the ideas and action of the leadership are the necessary expression of the irresistible will of the masses (which does, of course, not mean that all of their policies have been unwelcome to the masses), I find myself unable to appeal to the supposed knowledge about the masses which might derive from such a belief.

An even more serious charge which might be brought against these essays is not so much that they concern themselves with the behavior of the elite as that they treat the words—the "verbal behavior"—of the elite as one primary datum in explaining their "nonverbal behavior," instead of explaining all their policies in terms of our own superimposed social-scientific categories. Such a procedure runs counter to an overwhelming tendency in the American academy to dismiss what men say about their beliefs and intentions in explaining the real springs of their behavior. One proves one's profundity by discounting the conscious behavior of others. The explanation of their behavior must be sought in forces operating behind their backs, as these forces are defined by the social sciences (the American social sciences), cultural anthropology, depth psychology, "political culture," and so forth and so on.

It is not my intention here to enter into a lengthy philosophic disquisition on the relationship between behavior and conscious ideas expressed in words. Nor is it my intention to deny the profoundly problematic nature of this relationship. The problem of the relation of Marxist-Leninist-Maoist language to Communist behavior is indeed a dominant theme in almost every selection in this book. It is, however, a problem because the possibility that conscious ideas *may* influence behavior is not dogmatically rejected. Moreover, it is a problem that exists for you and me as much as it does for Lenin and Mao. When we dogmatically discount the operational consequences of the verbal assertions of others, we do so through the vehicle of our own verbal assertions.[1] We somehow manage to maintain a touching faith that our own conscious verbal descriptions of the world not only bear some relation to the way the world is, but even affect our own behavior in that world, in spite of the fact that we are as much determined by social, cultural, and psychological factors as anyone else. It may be argued that while the verbal assertions of others are unscientific, ours are based on scientific truth. I shall not enter here into the question of how many of our current social-scientific doctrines have really been "scientifically" verified, nor why "scientific" ideas must affect behavior more than nonscientific ideas. I would point out, however, that the truth or falsehood of an idea has nothing to do with the question of its influence on behavior. While sharing the view that much in Marxist-Leninist-Maoist ideology has been proven false, this leaves entirely open the question

[1] I need hardly point out that the systematic discounting of the verbal assertions of others in terms of one's own "science" is as much a feature of Marxism-Leninism as of American social sciences. One of the more hilarious aspects of the modern intellectual scene is that the world is full of proud philosophers who are all able to dismiss each others' conscious assertions and motives in terms of their own scientific categories.

8

of the degree and nature of its influence on the behavior of its advocates.

There are also the cruder partisans of the "tough-minded," power-interest school who would maintain that the political elites are entirely conscious of their lack of belief in their own ideological assertions but simply use ideological language to advance personal and national power interests. Stalin, some would assert, was perfectly well aware of the unreality of his own Marxist-Leninist formulations and used them quite consciously to advance the aims of power or security. Here again, one cannot deny that in the long history of mankind one may find political figures who seem to approximate this Machiavellian ideal type. Nor can one deny that all political leaders occasionally use specific ideological language in this knowingly manipulative way. By and large, however, it would be extremely naive to rely heavily on this crude model of the way in which ideas relate to power interests. Those who have possessed power have been quite as prone (if not more so) as others to believe that their power pursuits play a meaningful role in a larger, transcendental order of things. Far from being mutually exclusive, certain types of ideological claims and certain types of power interests reinforce and enhance each other. It is the absolutely pure power-operator who must be regarded as the rare freak.

A more sophisticated version of the power approach would simply disregard the question of the subjective commitment to ideas and beliefs by the power-holders. Power, it would argue, has its own, self-sufficient logic and dynamic. Whether one is dealing with power struggles among individuals, groups, or institutions, whether with domestic or international relations, one can explain all power behavior quite adequately in terms of the inner logic and dynamic of the power game itself. Here I would simply repeat what I state elsewhere in this volume, that there is no one logic of power and that the relations of ideas to power may assume infinite variations. The tendency may be to aggrandize power at all cost, to aggrandize power but to calculate soberly the risks involved, to conserve existing power, or even to yield power. The ideas, ideals, and beliefs in the heads of power-holders may be relevant to all these ways of handling power. The same ideas may at one time be an active spur to the pursuit of power and at other times become a mere rationalization of existent power. Within the same ideological complex, parts of the ideology may have a genuine channeling effect on the modalities of power, and may profoundly effect the response to given situations; other parts may become rationalization and ritual phraseology. The same complexity obtains in the relations among ideas, organizations, and institutions. Ideas may give rise to organizations that then become foci of social power. There are those who are prepared to maintain that organizations such as Communist parties, once they are launched, can simply live on as engines of power whatever may be the vicissitudes of the ideas on which they are presumably based and in terms of which they seek legitimization. This is, however, a proposition which bears much hard scrutiny. What we require above all else is a model of man that presents him in all his tragic complexity, as a creature who acts on the basis of ideas and goals, whose ideas and goals are enmeshed in countless ways with the pursuit of power and the preservation of interests, and who must respond to the demands of objective situations he has neither created nor anticipated.

Another objection which might be made to some of these writings is that they focus not on Chinese society or the Chinese historic process, but on the vicissitudes of a largely non-Chinese ideology and movement. In a sense this is the same issue, but viewed from a different angle. It is an undeniable fact that the conscious ideology of the Chinese

Communist leadership has been dominated by concepts which are mostly non-Chinese in origin. The cultural determinists—those who insist that everything the Chinese do and say must in some sense be irreducibly "Chinese" —must therefore systematically discount the non-Chinese element in the assertions of the Chinese Communist leadership. They must systematically reject the claims of the leadership that it is involved in a transnational, transcultural movement which still owes much to two foreigners named Marx and Lenin. To be sure, one might say that even conscious Communist ideology in China is constantly becoming more "Chinese." We are now told that the "Thought of Mao Tse-tung" is the highest realization of Marxism-Leninism in the twentieth century. This does not mean—it must be noted—that the Maoist group in China is in any way stressing its continuity with the Chinese past. On the conscious level this group still clings more convulsively than ever to the ecumenical transcultural significance of its ideas, which it claims are neither Western nor derived from the Chinese past but something new under the sun.

The problem of the relationship of contemporary Chinese society to Chinese culture of the past is certainly a fundamental question with which one must be profoundly concerned. Both the cultural and what might be called the "objective" heritage of the past (for example, the size of the peasant population) may in the long run have more to do with the shape of China's future than Marxist-Leninist Communism as we have known it. If the Chinese state continues in some sense to be a Communist state this Communism may, in the long run, be "Chinese" in many significant ways. There is nothing in the premises of these writings which would negate such a development. What I am concerned with here, however, is the present and the immediate past. After all, a concern with contemporary

11

affairs should, in the first instance, involve an effort to understand the present. Again it must be stressed that although the future of China will undoubtedly be shaped by an enormous variety of factors lying beyond the control of China's present leaders, we cannot pass them by in dealing with the present. If the cultural determinist is prepared to argue that, during the period under consideration in these writings, the Chinese Communist leaders did not regard themselves as participants in a transcultural world movement, did not take its notions as they understood them seriously, and did not act on the basis of and with reference to these notions, we must reject his dogmas. The concept of a culture or a society as a kind of hermetically sealed monad impervious to outside influences is not to my mind admissible. Throughout human history there have been transcultural religions and movements which have ruthlessly cut across cultures and profoundly modified them. (They have, of course, also been modified in turn.) I find no difficulty whatsoever in conceiving of Chinese who regard themselves as committed to movements and ideas which are not exclusively Chinese. They have existed in the past and are even more likely to exist in the future when all the cultures of mankind will be in constant and unavoidable communication with each other. The Chinese leadership must, of course, be studied within its Chinese context and frame of reference. It must also be studied within the context of the history of Marxist-Leninist Communism, to which it has claimed a commitment. This focus is particularly relevant to many of the problems considered in these essays.

If we reject prevailing dogmas concerning the relation of conscious "ideas in men's heads" to their behavior, we can then study only the concrete ways in which specific bodies of ideas and beliefs have been related to specific modes of behavior within the stream of time. One neither discounts words nor takes them at face value. Viewing the broad history of Marxist-Leninist Communism [2] from Lenin to such sundry figures as Mao Tse-tung, Tito, Brezhnev, Kosygin, Castro, and Gomulka, I would continue to maintain what may seem to some the paradoxical view that the general tendency has been toward the disintegration of Marxist-Leninist ideology, that ideology has continued to play a significant role even in the course of its disintegration, and that the disintegration is itself a fact with enormous consequences. To this I would add, however, that Marxism-Leninism has also become the carrier, the vehicle for the transmission, of more general and older notions of the Western radical tradition. These are statements which probably bear further defense and amplification.

The Dictatorship of the Proletariat: The History of a Phrase. The position adopted here can be clarified by placing it in juxtaposition to certain other widely held views on the evolution of Marxism-Leninism. There are the views which insist that after certain cut-off points in time the ideological tradition to which allegiance is claimed is no longer relevant to behavior. Social Democratic Marxists would claim that after Lenin's perversions of Marx, Marxism becomes irrelevant to the behavior of the Soviet Communists. There is the Trotskyist view that Stalinism has nothing to do with true Marxism-Leninism. The Maoist "Cultural Revolution," we are told, has nothing in common with authentic Marxist-Leninist doctrine; and so forth. The dialectic of disintegration as here conceived, however, does not recognize such absolute cut-off points. The process

2 The word "Communism" itself has, of course, been subject to enormous semantic confusions. The suffix "ism" suggests a body of ideas, but the word has been used by some to refer to the Soviet political and economic system in particular and by others to refer to the presumed ultimate goals of all who call themselves Communist—namely a Communist society. What we are concerned with here is that line of evolution which runs from Marx to Lenin-Stalin-Mao (and others) and the political movement with which these ideas have been associated.

of decay involves both continuities and discontinuities in complex combinations. Lenin transformed and tore asunder many elements of mature Marxism, yet his transformations must still be understood in relation to the Marxism which he espoused. Stalin may hardly have been an impassioned visionary, but his very position forced him to relate his behavior in some fashion to Marxist-Leninist ideology as he found it; the ideology itself was a factor of power. Mao Tse-tung's relationship to the Marxist-Leninist tradition remains an important aspect of his cast of mind as well as his behavior. We may now rapidly be approaching the hazy borderline area where it becomes questionable whether one can any longer speak of a common Communist ideology or movement in any sense. This is a question I shall consider further.

As a concrete illustration of the complex process under examination. I might dwell at somewhat greater length on the phrase "dictatorship of the proletariat," which is treated in a number of the essays in this volume. This phrase and its vicissitudes lie at the very heart of the evolution of Marxist-Leninist Communism. The phrase occurs only in passing in the later writings of Marx, and we will probably never know the concrete political meaning, if any, which he assigned to it. One can assume that he probably did not envisage anything like a Leninist party. Most probably he believed that the industrial workers as a class would themselves in some fashion play an active role in the coming socialist revolution. With Marx, the concept of the "proletariat" embraces two essential components. It refers to a specific socioeconomic class conceived of as the social bearer of certain transcendental, messianic tasks, and it refers to the syndrome of virtues and qualities which characterize this class. One of the most important attributes of the proletariat is, of course, its transnational, universal character.

With Lenin the phrase became the very keystone of the arch even while undergoing a drastic shift in meaning. It became the ideological foundation—the soul of the Communist Party. Dictatorship can be achieved only by a political organization designed to seize and maintain power. The Communist Party is that organization. As such it embodies all the transcendental qualities which Marx attributes to the proletariat. Its infallibility derives from the proletariat's "true consciousness" of the world; its total jurisdiction from the totality of the proletariat's mission; its monolithic unity from the proletariat's transcendence of self-interest; and its transnational nature from proletarian internationalism. The fact that authentic socialism can be achieved only by the Communist Party obviously reflects the mission of the working class. During the whole period from Lenin until just yesterday the essential faith of any uncoerced Communist was the faith that the world Communist movement centered in Moscow did indeed embody all of these transcendental proletarian virtues and capacities. It was not that the political organization had replaced the class. However clear it may be to the unbeliever that industrial workers played little role in the rise or survival of Soviet Communism, there is no reason to think that Lenin or even Stalin did not believe their own injunctions that the party must be in close contact with the working class. As a matter of fact where Communist parties became important in the West (for example, France and Italy), they did in fact establish a proletarian base. If the non-Communist Jean-Paul Sartre was persuaded that the French Communist Party was the authentic vanguard of the proletariat, this belief was plausibly supported by the French situation. To the convinced and uncoerced Western Communist the presumed real relationship of the party to the class remained a central living aspect of his faith.

It was in the Chinese Communist experience of the thir-

15

ties and forties that it became patently clear that the proletarian consciousness and proletarian virtue could become entirely divorced from their presumed class moorings and lodged in the political organization itself. While never baldly stated, the implications of this shift were clearly drawn during the Yenan period. The "proletarian nature" of the Chinese Communist Party was henceforth guaranteed, not by its relation to industrial workers (in spite of ritual phrases to this effect), but by its possession of a correct "proletarian attitude" and its abilities to inculcate those attitudes in its potential members. The "proletarian nature" had been almost totally sundered from its presumed socioeconomic bearer. A further consequence of this shift was what might be called its populist implication. If a proletarian education could itself create a proletarian party out of every variety of human material—peasants, students, and intellectuals—such education could be extended to create a "proletarian" disposition in vast numbers of the "people." One could hold out to broad strata of the population the promise that they too might come to possess those qualities of mind and heart which would allow them to participate in the "building of socialism." It was out of such considerations that the suggestion arose that China might achieve socialism with a "joint dictatorship" of the people under "proletarian" leadership rather than via a "dictatorship of the proletariat." As practical politics, the suggestion of such a possibility represented a sensible strategy in attracting elements who were frightened by the ominous phrase "dictatorship of the proletariat." It may also have reflected a "national populist" strain in Mao's own outlook. On the other hand, it represented a breach in the Soviet dogma that "dictatorship of the proletariat" provided the only path to socialism.

The first two of the following essays (No. 1 and No. 2) address themselves to this obscure, almost forgotten page in the dogmatic history of Communism. A case might be made for the contention that as far as the real internal political development of the Soviet Union, of Eastern Europe, and of China are concerned, these scholastic debates about the "dictatorship of the proletariat" had already become a matter of mere words even in the early fifties. Whether this was in fact the case, however, my own concern at the time was not with the debate as a reflection of domestic policies in the various states of the Communist bloc, but with its implications for the question of authority in the Communist bloc as a whole.

During the years in which these pieces were written (a period which now seems to belong to a forgotten past), the reality of Moscow's supreme authority in the Communist world was most palpably felt even though Tito's challenge to that authority had already taken place. Even in China this was the period of maximum Soviet ascendancy. All "hard" evidence seemed to indicate that Moscow's ideological authority in the Communist world was fully accepted in Peking. Peking seemed to support without reservation the facade of total unanimity which was the characteristic earmark of "proletarian internationalism." Monolithic unity seemed to be growing rather than diminishing. Nor was the evidence wholly ideological. As indicated in No. 2, "hard-headed" analysis of social political development within China, of economic relations between China and the bloc, of China's general international behavior, all tended to support the case of growing solidarity. The burden of proof rested heavily on those who doubted the solidity of Moscow's authority.

Was there any evidence whatsoever of Chinese resistance to total Soviet authority? My aim in these essays was to indicate that such evidence could be found in the Chinese handling of the concept of the "dictatorship of the proletariat." The Chinese had continued to maintain the sug-

17

gestion that China's achievement of socialism would not necessarily involve the dictatorship of the proletariat. From Moscow's point of view this implied a silent resistance to what was still considered to be a universal truth of Marxism-Leninism. It thus involved a muted challenge to Moscow's unquestioned authority to differentiate universal truths from particular truths. What is more, the substantive doctrine that socialism could be achieved only under the dictatorship of the proletariat was itself, from Moscow's point of view, an indispensable Leninist dogma. It implied that genuine "socialism" could be achieved only by Communist parties recognized by Moscow. Any implication that other political groups might collaborate in or carry out the achievement of socialism was a threat to Moscow's monopoly of access to the socialist future, and it was precisely this monopoly which created the qualitative abyss between the world of the redeemed and of the unredeemed.

An interesting confirmation of the reality of this debate is provided in a revealing speech delivered by Otto Kuusinen, formerly one of Stalin's close collaborators, in 1964, after the facade of Sino-Soviet unanimity had decisively crumbled. The Chinese, he bitterly complains, had concocted the notion of a "dictatorship of the people which had nothing in common with Marxism-Leninism," probably in order to "facilitate their game with the International bourgeoisies of other countries . . . March with us the leaders of Peking seemed to say to these elements and we will see to it that you are given a respectable place in the system of dictatorship which we have thought up." [3]

[3] Speech of Otto Kuusinen at the Plenum of the Central Committee of the CPSU, Feb. 1964; published in *Pravda*, May 19, 1964. Also, see Helene Carrere d'Encausse and Stuart Schram, *Le Marxisme et l'Asie*, Collection U (Paris: Armand Colin, 1965), pp. 462–475, esp. pp. 463, 464.

Oddly enough, however, the next turn in the history of dogma is marked by a dramatic reversal of attitude on the part of the Chinese in 1956, as pointed out in No. 2. The Chinese leaders pronounced their total conversion to the universal necessity of a "dictatorship of the proletariat," and in the ensuing decade the phrase was used with more and more vehemence, reaching a climax in 1966 when it became one of the key phrases of the doctrine of the Cultural Revolution. Does this argue for the decay of doctrine? Does it not rather support the notion that China has become the bastion of recrudescent orthodoxy? In fact, however, the relation between words and realities continues to pursue an erratic course of its own.

In 1956 the Khrushchev leadership in the Soviet Union, cheerfully believing that Soviet authority was compatible with some degree of autonomy in the bloc, had loosened the meaning of the phrase "dictatorship of the proletariat" sufficiently to embrace the Chinese concept of "the people's democratic dictatorship," thus conceding China a recognition of its difference while saving the vital phrase. The Chinese, in turn, accepted the universal necessity of the dictatorship of the proletariat. In retrospect, the explanation of this acceptance offered in No. 2 seems somewhat insufficient. The prospect that Peking would now begin to play a role in guiding the common affairs of the Communist bloc, together with a certain apprehension induced by Khrushchev's "Secret Speech" on Stalin, may have led Mao, Liu, and others to a new appreciation of the symbolic weight of the phrase (whatever its concrete political context) as a divider marking off the world of darkness from the world of light.

In effect what has happened in China since 1957 is that the Maoist group in particular has come to use this phrase with ever-increasing vehemence as a designation of the dominance of the forces of good—whatever these forces may

19

be—over the forces of evil, however defined. "Proletarian nature" now refers to a cluster of virtues, such as selfless submission to the collectivity, simplicity, austerity, unflagging energy, and single-minded hatred of the enemy, which can be thought of in detachment not only from its presumed class basis, but even from the Communist Party itself. One of the striking features of the Cultural Revolution is that the Communist Party is no longer the exclusive or even the most reliable bearer of the "proletarian dictatorship." Red Guards, the People's Liberation Army, and the inchoate Revolutionary Committees have now become the chief pillars of the dictatorship, and bourgeois corruption has been found at the very heart of the party. It seems difficult to believe that even the Maoist group in China is prepared to shunt aside the party permanently as the organized bearer of the proletarian essence. The group's own history is, after all, deeply involved with the mystique of the party, and it must still hope to create new "Marxist-Leninist" parties in the third world.[4] Yet there can be little doubt that the party as an organization has been seriously desacralized.

The proletarian dictatorship is exercised by whatever groups or individuals behave in what Mao conceives to be a proper proletarian way. All men harbor bourgeois proclivities within their own breasts and must learn with the help of Mao's Thoughts to overcome them. "Class struggle" now figures more prominently in the rhetoric of the Cultural Revolution than it ever has before, and the superficial reader might well conclude that China is involved in a classical Marxist struggle to the death between a bour-

---

[4] The logic of this development has been carried much further by Castro and Debray, the theoretician of Castroism. Here there is a positive rejection of the role of the bureaucratic party in bringing about revolution and an insistence that it is the revolution itself which must create the revolutionaries.

geoisie and proletariat. In fact "bourgeoisie" and "proletariat" have been transmuted in the Maoist universe into something like two pervasive fluids, one noxious and the other beneficial, which can find their lodgments anywhere. The source of the proletarian truth resides in no group or even organization but in the thought of Mao Tse-tung. Landlords, rich peasants, and others figure as actors in Mao's writings, but the real focus of bourgeois perfidy is to be found at the very heart of the Chinese Communist Party. Army, government, *and party* have all become the battlegrounds on which the proletarian and bourgeois essences fight out their battles. In fact, the ultimate battleground is the human soul—at least the souls of those who are to be the elite of virtue in the good society of the future. Every man must purge his own bourgeois ego. "Every man must make himself a revolutionary force and at the same time regard himself as an object of the revolution." [5] Having set out from a world view which finds the sources of human evil in man's distorted social relations, one has by a circuitous route returned to an honorable and ancient view of man found in many religions and philosophies: that the major battleground of good and evil is within the soul of man, in this case of those men who are to be the moral elite of the society (The Proletarian Revolutionary Faction).

What then remains of the link between Mao and Marx? Obviously many terms have survived. "Class struggle," "bourgeoisie," "proletariat," and "dictatorship of the proletariat" have never appeared with greater frequency than now. However much the particular truths of Maoism may be pushed into the foreground, there remains a kind of

[5] "Cheng-chüeh tui-tai tzu-chi" (On correctly dealing with oneself) in *Wuch'an chieh-chi Ko-ming-p'ai ta lien-ho ti hao hsing-shih*, Hsüeh-hsi Ts'ung-shu no. 10 (The good prospects for the great proletarian revolutionary alliance, study materials no. 10), Hong Kong, 1967.

21

instinctive realization that the universalistic, messianic claims of Peking cannot be utterly sundered from certain key terms of the older Marxist-Leninist vocabulary. If there is any substantive rather than verbal link, it is with the side of Marx that sees history in terms of a gigantic moral engagement fought out on a global scale between the forces of good and the forces of evil. Such a view of history hardly originated with Marx and is assuredly fully present in certain trends of thought arising out of the French Revolution. What Marx actually contributed in his mature doctrine was his specifically Marxist definition of the nature of the forces of evil and good as organically linked to an analysis of the forces of economic growth—the "forces of production." The Marxist labels have in China been preserved, but content has gone its own way.

The Leninist component of Marxism-Leninism has also become questionable. The suggestion that the "dictatorship of the proletariat" is not necessarily incarnate in the sacred body of the Communist Party, which is as subject to corruption as any other organized sector of the state (a suggestion which may not, to be sure, survive the more extreme phases of the Cultural Revolution; Chinese Communist history is, after all, deeply tied to the sanctioned history of the party), strikes at the doctrine of the party which might be called the very core of Leninism. It reflects the genuine suspicion of the aging Mao that Communist parties as now constituted, including his own Chinese Communist Party, have been weighed and found wanting as instruments for achieving his particular vision of the good society.

I have dwelt at some length on the career of the phrase "dictatorship of the proletariat," first, because it lies at the very heart of Leninist Communism and second, because it illustrates the complexity of the process of ideological decay with which we are concerned.

It must be stressed that I am not discussing here the subject of the decay of "ideology" as such, but the specific evolution of Marxist-Leninist ideology. I am by no means asserting that Marxist-Leninist ideology is giving way everywhere to the "end of ideology." In the China of the Cultural Revolution the *furor ideologicus* of Maoism rages more fiercely than ever, even though China has by no means become the home of true Marxism-Leninism. It would be enormously presumptuous to predict what must ultimately take the place of Marxist-Leninist assumptions in Rumania or Poland or even among those elements of French and Italian society which now vote Communist.

What I am asserting, however, is that the decay of Marxism-Leninism is of central relevance to the fate of what has been known since the October Revolution as "world Communism." "World Communism" (or now "Asian Communism," which presumably means a world Communism centered in Peking) as an entity still figures in official U.S. Government documents and media of communications. What is more, it is treated as an object of foreign policy decisions. Thus the question is hardly one of mere theoretical concern.

On Non-ideological Definitions of Communism. There are many broad ways of defining "Communism" which reject the "narrow" insistence on ideology. For instance, there are those who assert that "Communism" (at times they even use the word "Marxism" interchangeably with Communism) is not an ideology but a political or economic development which will inevitably emerge at a given phase of the "modernization process" or which will most probably emerge unless prevented. It is curious that one can arrive through such reasoning at diametrically opposed positions. One may accept Robert Heilbroner's view that Communism is an unpleasant but inevitable stage of eco-

23

nomic development, or one can take the view that we must intervene directly to prevent an otherwise inevitable triumph of Communism throughout Asia, Africa, or Latin America.

It is, of course, impossible to legislate the use of language. Terms such as Communism may be used as one sees fit, but all those who use "Communism" in the context of the present are no doubt prepared to see an immediate link drawn in the minds of their audience between that usage and the history of the particular movement which grew out of the October Revolution.

The notion that Communism is to be identified with a certain "Stalinist" model of economic development has, I think, already been exploded within the Communist world itself. I shall not dwell on the fact that the Stalinist model of industrial development did not exist at the time of Lenin's death or that many of the present leading figures of Chinese Communism had become Marxist-Leninists long before the Stalinist model of forced-draft industrialization had even appeared as a small cloud on the horizon. It would be entirely fallacious and totally anachronistic to assert that the founding fathers of Chinese Communism discovered in the Communism of 1921 a model of forced-draft industrialization.[6] What is more, the Chinese Communists have radically departed from the Soviet model since 1956–1957. Both the Great Leap Forward and the economic policies of the post-1960 period represent striking departures from the

[6] It can be maintained that the attraction of the Stalinist model of economic development has nowhere been the cause of the rise of strong Communist parties. Where strong Communist parties exist in the West their roots have been pre-Stalinist. The heart of their faith is the belief that the Soviet Union was finding not the path to development but the path to socialism and Communism. Similarly, where strong Communist tradition exists in Latin America and Asia, the roots go back to the early twenties. Here, of course, the attraction of the Leninist theory of imperialism must also be given considerable weight.

Stalinist pattern. The impact of the present Cultural Revolution on the economy is far from clear, but the most striking fact about the China of 1968 is that it has *not yet found* its definitive model of economic development. It is indeed by no means clear that the Soviet model of economic development is feasible in countries of overwhelmingly large peasant populations. Nor is it even clear that any "Communist" model which finally crystallizes in China will prove a totally irresistible model throughout the non-Western world.

A more serious "non-ideological" definition of Communism would stress the model of the one-party totalitarian state as an agent of forced modernization. Such states are depicted either as representing the "spread of Communism" or as halfway houses to Communism. Now, although the practice of one-party organization in the non-Western world has been profoundly influenced by the Soviet model, it has by no means been proven (1) that one-party states are more inevitable in the non-Western world than various other forms of polity (military dictatorships, for instance); or (2) that where they exist, they are all effective agents of forced modernization or even that they are effectively able to enforce the type of totalitarianism which was one of the striking products of Marxism-Leninism. Furthermore, although their conceptions of party have been profoundly influenced by Moscow, their populist Jacobin ideologies reach behind Marx and Lenin to the French Revolution. They could have found their ideology if Communism had never existed.

The heart of Marxist-Leninist Communism is to be sought not in that which it has shared with all the one-party states that have emerged in Africa, Asia, and Latin America, but precisely in that which differentiates it from them. The mystique of the Communist Party lies not in its organizational structure but in its transcendental status as the incarnation of the will of History and in its universal, messianic, "proletarian" mission. From this stems its claim of infallibility and utter disinterestedness. It was this that provided the sanction for totalitarian intervention in every corner of life. It was this that provided the sanction for unlimited terror. It was also this which provided the basis for the international authority of Moscow in the world Communist movement. Where Moscow's authority did not rest on sheer physical coercion, this mystique provided its foundation. The ideology itself was an essential ingredient of power. Genuine conversion to Communism and unquestioning acceptance of Moscow's directives by Communists abroad was based precisely on faith in the metaphysical status of the Communist Party.

Viewed in this light, it becomes readily apparent that the "international" crisis of the Communist movement cannot go hand in hand with the continued existence of stable "national Communisms." As stressed in essay No. 5, when each Communist party possesses the full authority to "extend and apply" the "universal truths" of Marxism-Leninism, it is by no means clear that any universal truths will survive. If the notion of an indivisible (not indivisible in the sense that there must be one "path to socialism" but in the sense that there must be no other authority which can sanction the legitimacy of a given "path to socialism") universal Marxist-Leninist truth no longer exists in "intra-bloc" relations, it also becomes questionable as applied to party authority within any given national society. In fact, Communist parties everywhere find themselves in a state of acute crisis within their own national societies. The CPSU itself is in a state of profound uncertainty about the extent to which it can maintain its totalitarian role in Soviet society. Nor can the Cultural Revolution in China be considered wholly apart from this general crisis of the Communistic movement. The CPSU may survive the crisis in some form by finding the main source of its legitimacy in "Soviet patriotism" and by identifying itself as the sponsor of "modernization." Such a Communist party will probably have to find its basis in a much more limited and uncertain authoritarianism. In China, on the other hand, the Maoists, having become aware that Communist parties as such (including the CCP leadership with its blatant resistance to Mao's "cultural" policies) are no longer capable of incarnating their version of the transcendent "proletarian truth," have been seeking true "proletarian revolutionaries" outside of the framework of the party. A much more explicit desanctification of the party organization as such can, of course, be found in the Castroist ideology of Regis Debray. If the one-party states are halfway houses to Communism, Marxist-Leninist Communism has itself proved a halfway house in the first instance—to the triumph of the nation-state and thereafter to a completely unknown future.

I shall not dwell here on that particular argument which minimizes the enormity of the crisis in the Communist world by insisting that no matter how they may differ in their strategies and interests, all Communists share the same ultimate goal of a "Communist society." As suggested in the eighth essay, the very nature of the goal itself is defined by the party or the leader, and there now exists an enormous gulf between the present Chinese "Maoist" conception of Communist society and what the Maoists call Soviet "goulash" Communism. It may be true that all Communist states will continue to share the common denominator of the state's preponderant role in economic life, but we are already fully aware of the enormous variety of economic developments which can take place within the framework of a "nationalized" economy. To the type of anti-Communist who regards the mere existence of states with such nationalized economies as an intolerable threat to his existence, there is nothing further to be said. To those whose fear of Marxist-Leninist Communism in the forties and fifties was based on the sense of a threat from a monolithic, organized world movement both willing and able to impose its totalitarian will on others, the cataclysmic crisis which has shaken that movement must make all the difference in the world.

On Cold War Revisionism and Dogmatism. If our view of the evolution of Communism must reject "non-ideological" definitions of Communism which find the heart of the matter in specific economic models or specific forms of political organization or vague common goals, it is also resistant to a "Cold War revisionism" which insists that the cold war was "all our fault." I shall not dwell on that particular form of "revisionism" which revives the view that the American social structure is inherently imperialistic while Communist social structures are "inherently" nonimperialistic. The issues involved would carry us too far afield. Most generally, one might raise the question whether any "social system" as such is inherently one or the other. Without denying for a moment the possibility that the United States has been or can be imperialistic, I shall simply voice the opinion that the reasons conventionally offered for the inherently nonexpansionist nature of the Soviet or Chinese "system" seem to me extraordinary feeble. What will concern us here are views such as the following: that it should have always been obvious to us (1) that Stalin was concerned only with national security, (2) that Marxism-Leninism as an ideology held no expansionist threat, and (3) that Moscow could never maintain a monolithic control of foreign Communist states and parties. Two of these contentions are again based on the notion that ideological "words" are never to be taken seriously, while a third seems to me to be based on an innocuous and erroneous interpretation of Marxist-Leninist-Stalinist ideology during the period in question.

Terms such as "national interest" and "security" are, as we know, everywhere notoriously labile. Nor is it at all easy to distinguish clearly security, power, ambition, and ideology. There can be no doubt that Stalin identified the interests of Marxism-Leninism with his own interpretation of the interests of the Soviet state. Why should he not also have believed his own assertions that the Soviet state was the bastion and spearhead of Marxism-Leninism? Why should he not have believed that he himself was the bearer of a historic mission to advance the interests of the "Socialist Camp" wherever he deemed it possible? Was there anything in such a belief which would have run counter to his self-image? If his dominant motive was an overpowering passion for personal and national security, what were his requirements for security? Did they not include among the minimum prerequisites the absolute control from Moscow of an international Communist movement which in the years immediately following World War II seemed to face brilliant prospects in both Western Europe and Asia?

It has been maintained that had it not been for cold war moves initiated by the United States, the Kremlin might not have attempted to impose a full Soviet system in Eastern Europe. It is true that between the years 1945–1948 there was some concern in Moscow with the problem of finding a broader base of support for the new East European governments. The result was the notion of "people's democracy" discussed in essay No. 1. As indicated, however, there was no thought whatsoever from the very outset of doing without "proletarian hegemony" (effective Communist Party control) or without effective control from Moscow of the Communist parties themselves. As we know from the famous secret speech on Stalin, Tito's challenge to Moscow's authority produced a traumatic shock of incredulity. It also is quite clear that during the whole period from 1949 until Stalin's death, enormous pressures

29

were brought to bear to establish the ascendancy of Moscow's authority in China within the limits imposed by Chinese conditions. The fact that Stalin was occasionally willing to sacrifice the interests of a local Communist party to the expediencies of Soviet foreign policy does not prove that he did not cherish high hopes for an active international Communist movement monolithically controlled from Moscow. It rather reflected his supreme confidence that such behavior would not shake the faith of uncoerced believers who would automatically identify Soviet interest with those of the "Socialist Camp."

The notion that Marxist-Leninist ideology in itself does not have expansionist implications is still often urged on the grounds that "Marxism" stresses the ultimacy of "spontaneous" impersonal forces in bringing about revolution. It seems odd that it must still be pointed out that Leninism is precisely characterized by its lack of faith in spontaneous forces and its reliance on "subjective" forces. It may be true, as the Chinese insist, that the Soviet Union has now returned to a reliance on "objective" economic forces ("Kautskyism" in Chinese terminology), yet it would be quite erroneous to think that this has become the exclusive content of Soviet ideology.[7] Moscow is even now probably entirely prepared to support Moscow-oriented Communist parties in the most abysmally undeveloped areas if it can find them.

It has also been urged that Leninism itself did not im-

[7] The present Soviet emphasis on industrial development, on "demonstrative" economic competition, may mark a return to a faith in "objective historic forces" but not necessarily a return to "orthodox Marxism." The notion of the primacy of objective economic forces is by no means uniquely Marxist and is fully shared by the American ideology of the "process of industrialization." It is a tendency of thought which is both older and broader than Marxism. Mature Marxism must be defined in terms of Marx's concrete analysis of these forces.

ply "subversion from without" (that is, from outside the national society) but revolution by the "proletarian forces" from within. However, during the whole period from the twenties to the fifties of this century, it was entirely reasonable to expect that national Communist parties would without question act on directives from Moscow (even the effort to prove that such was not necessarily the case in China involved enormous methodological difficulties). This was the very substance of "proletarian internationalism." What is more, there was nothing in the Leninist outlook which precluded direct intervention, under conditions deemed to be favorable, by Soviet forces on the side of "progressive" forces within a given state. Such an intervention, as in the case of Hungary, would not be "external." It would merely be a case of the whole "international proletariat" supporting a part.[8] The dialectics of externality and internality thus provided no ground for discounting the threat of a Soviet expansionism justified in ideological terms and based on the supreme ideological authority of the Kremlin.

It is true that one of the mitigating, countervailing, and historically fortunate aspects of the Leninist heritage has been Lenin's own cautious insistence that action be based on a sober analysis of "objective situations." The analysis of "objective situations" has always ostensibly been based on Marxist-Leninist categories, but behind these categories there generally lay the sorts of consideration of political and military realities which have always animated cautious statesmen and politicians everywhere. It is a noteworthy

[8] The Vietnamese war has unfortunately proven that the juggling of the categories of "externality" and "internality" is not peculiar to the Communist world. In that world, the Hungarian revolution was interpreted in Soviet literature as intervention from without while the Soviet intervention was simply in support of the resistance of the "masses" from within.

31

fact that both Stalin and Mao Tse-tung have in the main carried on this tradition of caution in their external policies. One need not doubt that they have both genuinely believed that History would, in the fullness of time, create more and more favorable objective situations, but neither has been markedly "adventuristic." Caution, however, has never implied indifference to favorable opportunities (such as those which lay behind the Korean War). For the most part such opportunities were to be sought and exploited through the instrumentality of the existing international Communist movement and not through the direct commitment of the resources of the Soviet state.

It is precisely this fact, however, which points to the enormity of the crisis that has engulfed the Communist world. At the heart of this crisis, as is argued in the fifth essay, lies the collapse of Moscow's authority and the disintegration of "proletarian internationalism." This does not mean that Communist regimes in Eastern Europe, which find themselves caught in an agonizing contradiction between efforts to establish a broad basis of support within their own societies and the presumably "Marxist-Leninist" basis of their authority, may not find it expedient to align themselves with the Soviet Union on many international issues. Nor does it mean that the Soviet government of Kosygin and Brezhnev no longer dreams of the restoration of Moscow's authority. I would be prepared to argue (1) that the collapse of Moscow's ideological authority as it existed in the past is irreversible, and (2) that Peking, having played an aggressive role in the subversion of this central mystery of Communism, will not be able to reconstitute it under its own auspices. When Moscow in the past issued grandiose pronouncements on the strategy of the world Communist movements, it counted on the existence of a panoply of Communist parties and states ready to do everything possible to implement its directives. When Lin Piao issued his statement on People's Liberations Wars in 1965 (see No. 8), he had little reason to believe that there existed anywhere, except possibly in Albania, reliable groups prepared to implement Peking's directive without hesitation. Thus, in spite of the enormous Maoist emphasis on the "subjective factor," one finds that Lin Piao's statement must place an unusual degree of reliance on the forces of History to create situations favorable not only to the implementation of Maoist strategy of revolution but to the creation of "true Marxist-Leninist" vanguards.

To maintain that it should always have been obvious that the ideological authority of Moscow was not real and would not endure is to engage in what might be called fraudulent hindsight. To be sure, some of those who insisted most fanatically on the monolithic solidity of the bloc were prepared to say that "someday" this solidity might collapse, but they were equally insistent that this someday was so far off that it should not be allowed to intrude as a real consideration in the making of foreign policy. There were those who seriously doubted the strength and durability of Communist transnational authority, who found in both the Chinese and Yugoslav experiences important evidence that this authority would not endure, and who felt that the collapse of bloc solidarity should figure as a real variable in projecting policies. It would be utterly false, however, to maintain that the obvious "solid" evidence supported them. The total surface consensus of Communist media seemed to support not only those who emphasized the unflagging power of Communist ideology—but, as indicated in the third essay, was used by many who discounted the ideological factor. The solidarity of totalitarian elites, the growing economic interdependence, direct military control (in Eastern Europe), the

33

susceptibility of underdeveloped countries to Communist manipulation, the growing "Sovietization" of China, all argued for bloc solidarity and expansionism.

The common link which binds the cold war revisionist and the cold war dogmatist is the failure to take seriously the enormity of the present crisis in the Communist world. They share a static view of the history of Communism. If it has become clear that the transnational claims of Communism have not prevailed, it is clear to the revisionist that they were never real. If something like a "Communist world" once existed, it is clear to the dogmatist that either it is still there or it is about to be reconstituted under the aegis of Peking.

Why Disintegration? If the assertion is valid that the general tendency has been toward the disintegration of Marxist-Leninist ideology and that ideology has continued to be of basic importance even in its process of disintegration, something should be said on the question of why this may be so. Until not long ago, it was quite common to find comparisons drawn between the rise of Marxist-Leninist Communism and the emergence of Christianity in the late Roman Empire. The implication was clear that we were dealing with a millennial movement which would transform human history for centuries to come. It may even now be argued that just as Christianity could accommodate the rise of Roman Catholicism, Greek Orthodoxy, and post-Reformation Protestantism without ceasing to be "Christianity," Communism can be defined sufficiently broadly to embrace Maoism and Titoism, the doctrines of Togliatti and of Ch'en Po-ta. Hence, the organizational disarray of Communism is no proof of its debility.

The question which concerns us here is not whether Mao Tse-tung, Tito, Castro, and Togliatti all have the "right" to call themselves true Marxist-Leninists, but whether Communism in all its guises and manifestations is analogous in historic significance to Christianity. What I shall suggest is that Marxist-Leninist Communism in general marks not so much the beginning of a vast new historic epoch as the end of an age of absolute sociopolitical faiths.[9] In speaking of the disintegration of Marxism-Leninism, I do not mean to suggest that Western liberalism and Western types of social democracy *as all-embracing creeds* are in a state of flourishing health. On all sides absolute sociopolitical truths are being relativized and being shown to be of more limited significance than originally proclaimed.[10]

Nor is it my intention merely to assert that the truth claims of Marxism-Leninism have, on the whole, not been justified. It will be immediately pointed out that religious philosophies and movements deemed untrue by many have flourished for centuries. What I would like to assert, however, is that Marxism-Leninism as a creed suffers from the sheer excessiveness of its claims. Unlike the church to which it has often been compared, the Communist Party (the World Communist movement) has not simply been the bearer of certain eternal, unchanging verities. Its voice is the voice of History incarnate, but History, unlike eternal timeless truths, unfolds in the emerging present. One of the main assumptions of Leninism has been that the whole path of development from the past to the future was not spelled out in the single revelation of Marx's *Capital*. His-

9 This does not mean, of course, that we may not yet become involved in a holocaust carried on in the name of these faiths.

10 There is no reason to believe that the decline of these sociopolitical faiths must lead to the triumph of that type of "end of ideology" which now proclaims that all significant human problems are about to be solved by a kind of "social scientific" technocracy. Nor does the rise of the "new radicalism" necessarily contradict my thesis. The fate of Marxism-Leninism is certainly not to be equated with the fate of radicalism as a broad tendency. However, the new radicalism seems more a pathos than an ideology. Whether it will be able to create new absolute ideologies seems to me more than doubtful.

tory is full of twists and turns, shoals and eddies, and only the "proletarian" party knows how to apply the "universal truths" to the situations which emerge in given times and places. The party thus dispenses absolute, infallible truths concerning the temporal flux of events. It speaks with equal authority about Asia, Africa, or the United States of America. Furthermore, since History in the Hegelian-Marxist interpretation embraces the whole of human life within its precincts, the party must proclaim infallible truths concerning both "substructural" and "superstructural" matters. This is the foundation of its totalitarian authority. The infallibility of the party is furthermore never sullied by the distorting perspectives of individual or group self-interest.

The mere fact that proletarian transcendence had become tied to the destiny of one super-nation-state was not sufficient in itself to shake the appeal of Marxist-Leninist truth claims during the period before the end of World War II, although the suspicion that the "party line" served Soviet national interests was an important source of disaffection even during that period.

To Stalinist believers, however, the power of the Soviet Union provided both solace and tangible support of the validity of their creed. "Socialism in one country" when applied to the Soviet case implied not simply singularity but uniqueness. The Soviet Union was a unique, sacred kingdom from which radiated the supreme, undivided authority of living Communist truth. Nothing could have been further from Stalin's mind than the notion that the single-country socialism of the Soviet Union should provide the model for other states, that Communist parties in these states should enjoy the authority in their own societies which the CPSU enjoyed in the Soviet Union. This reflected not only Stalin's inordinate jealousy of power but also a realization that the authority underlying the kind of truth claims made by Moscow could not be shared. Total infallibility and the identification of "proletarian internationalism" with the interests of the Soviet Union were indivisible attributes.

In fact, the main challenge to the overweening moral and intellectual claims of Moscow was to come not from enemies outside but from Communist movements which had attained state power—in the first instance from movements which had created their own power and secondly even from Communist leaderships that had been imposed by Moscow. The claims made by Mao Tse-tung during the Yenan period that he had himself forged the connection between the universal truths of Marxism-Leninism and the particularities of the Chinese situation did not merely reflect his own ideological ambitions but also a practical experience which brought into question Moscow's "Leninist" infallibility in coping with Chinese actualities. One must assume that when the CCP came to power in 1949 the Chinese leadership had something less than a full faith in Moscow's universal infallibility, that it was already determined to exercize autonomy (on the Soviet analogy) within its own society, but that it genuinely believed that shared assumptions and shared common interests would transcend all else.

In the case of Tito, the heart of the crisis involved a growing disbelief on the part of the Yugoslav leadership in the absolute "proletarian" purity of Soviet motives and a growing suspicion that Soviet interests were not identical with "proletarian internationalism." [11] The other side of this coin was, of course, Tito's burning conviction that the survival of his own leadership was by no means incompatible with "proletarian internationalism."

The most crucial moment in this crisis of the Communist world occurred during the period 1957–1960, when the

---

11 The Yugoslav letters, in the exchange between Moscow and Belgrade in 1948, provide an almost touching testimonial of the degree to which the Yugoslav Communist leadership had previously accepted the Kremlin's moral claims.

leadership of the Chinese Communist Party discovered that the spiritual authority of the CPSU was not only questionable as it pertained to Chinese matters but could no longer be accepted as infallible or disinterested in bloc polices as a whole. One conceivable outcome of all this might have been a movement to the kind of Communist federation discussed in No. 3 and No. 5. Here again the excessive claims of the Marxist-Leninist conception of spiritual authority have made such an outcome unlikely. Shared assumptions have not prevented the emergence of wide differences of opinion on general bloc policy. These differences of opinion have proven incompatible with the convention of total consensus, and the convention of total consensus is inseparable from the claim of infallibility. Furthermore, if the authority to apply the universal truths of Marxism-Leninism to any specific national society now belongs to national Communist parties, the extraordinary authority which the party enjoys to reinterpret and "creatively apply" its own universal truths is now fragmented among a host of national parties whose own interests and particular national situations impel them to call into question more and more universal truths. At the heart of the Sino-Soviet polemic, on its ideological side, we find well-grounded mutual accusations that each side has undermined essential universal truths of Marxism-Leninism. The Chinese Communist leadership has by no means opted for a federalist solution in spite of its striking insistence that the authority of each Communist party be confined to the national jurisdiction of that party. This doctrine operates on the formalistic constitutional level and is used as a weapon against the claims of the CPSU. On a deeper level, the Maoist leadership remains profoundly and even frenetically committed to the Marxist-Leninist mystery of authority. "Proletarian" authority has departed from Moscow but, like a sacred irradiant cloud, it has descended, one and indivisible, onto the palaces of Peking. Whether the effulgence remains is a question to be considered.

On China as the Center of Marxist-Leninist Truth. I have so far concentrated on the evolution of Marxist-Leninist Communism as a world movement with transcultural claims and treated China only in relation to this movement. Since the Chinese at present claim that the epicenter of this movement now rests in Peking, it is essential to focus our attention finally on China itself.

As indicated in the final essay, the fact that Peking is now revealed as the center of Communist truth has enormously reinforced the opinions of those who have always felt that Chinese events must be viewed wholly within a Chinese framework. The question of whether Russian culture has or has not been part of or "affiliated" with the culture of the West remains unanswered. But there can be no doubt about the separate evolution of Chinese culture. Furthermore, even if one takes seriously the revolutionary nature of the changes which have taken place in China during the last century, it remains a revolution within a Chinese historic process. The Chinese Communist Party could achieve power only by relating itself to the objective realities of Chinese realities, and the leaders themselves have emerged out of a Chinese experience. Maoism is basically a Chinese product, and its relations to the world movement we have been discussing here have always been marginal and superficial. The center of Chinese Communism has not finally settled in Peking; it never really left.

A somewhat modified version of this view of Maoism would see in it the offspring of a marriage between Marxism-Leninism and the Chinese revolution, but an offspring which must be treated as an individual in its own right. Chinese Communism, whatever its relationship to the history of Marxism-Leninism, is a new and independent factor in the world—a factor operating within a discrete Chinese historic process. If there is a process of disintegration taking place in the Marxist-Leninist tradition, this need bear no relationship to the future course of Chinese Communism. Furthermore, even if my hypothesis that the age of absolute sociopolitical ideologies may be drawing to a close in the West (here including Eastern Europe and the Soviet Union) is valid, this may by no means be true of China.

I have no quarrel with the proposition that the future course of Chinese history may be more decisively shaped by "Chinese" factors than by the impact of Marxism-Leninism. I am concerned here, however, not with the evolution of China past and future, but with the Maoist development of Chinese Communism. It may also be conceded that the evolution of Maoism itself has been shaped in many of its most vital aspects by Chinese conditions and by unconscious cultural habits inherited from the past. The issue here is whether the destiny of Maoism is or is not still implicated with the destiny of Marxism-Leninist Communism. It is not merely a question of whether Mao and his group *can* extricate themselves from an involvement with the history of Marxism-Leninism, it is a question of whether they *desire* to do so. The striking slogan of the Cultural Revolution, that Maoism is the highest expression of Marxism-Leninism in the twentieth century, highlights on the one hand the enormity of Mao's claims as a prophet to mankind, and on the other hand the fact that these claims are still made in the name of Marxism-Leninism rather than in the name of an entirely new Maoist faith.

One might indeed ask—why is Maoism *tout court* not proclaimed as the new faith of twentieth century revolution? It will by no means do to reply that Mao still shares with Kosygin and Brezhnev the goal of a Communist society. One of the most vehemently proclaimed doctrines of the Cultural Revolution is that Mao's vision of the Communist society has practically nothing in common with the "goulash" Communism of the Soviet Union.[12] Until the Cultural Revolution, one might have stated (see No. 7) that the crucial role of the Communist Party in Chinese society was inseparable from its Marxist-Leninist rationale. Yet at least the Maoist group in China now seems prepared to devalue and diminish the role of the party as such on the grounds that as an institution it has proven as corruptible as every other organ of society.

If we then ask ourselves what the heart of the matter is, we again find ourselves driven to those familiar terms—proletariat, dictatorship of the proletariat, and bourgeoisie. As already suggested, it is these terms which evidently symbolize in Mao's mind his vital link to the whole Marxist-Leninist tradition. While some of China's most ardent admirers in the "revolutionary" left abroad have drawn from the Chinese experience the conclusion that the peasantry and the poor have now inherited the messianic task which Marx assigned to the industrial proletariat, and see in this the new gospel of the Chinese revolution, Mao himself has never drawn this conclusion. In spite of the role of the peasantry in the Chinese revolution, in spite of the strain in Maoism toward a populist-nationalist formula, Mao has never attributed to the peasantry or the poor as such the transcendent virtues and capacities suggested by the word "proletariat." Indeed, to the present day we can still find in Chinese Communist literature all the Marxist clichés about the weaknesses of the peasantry. If the industrial workers as such have failed to manifest the proletarian nature assigned to them by Marx, this does not mean that this nature inheres in the peasantry or any other socioeco-

[12] That is, nothing beyond the state ownership of the means of production which in Mao's view is entirely compatible with bourgeois degeneration.

41

nomic segmentation of the society.[13] The peasantry does not possess proletarian virtue, it is merely capable of proletarianization through Maoist education.

To be sure, if the proletarian nature does not inhere in a socioeconomic class, it has become more than doubtful since the Cultural Revolution whether it inheres in the Communist Party as such. One might indeed say that aside from the person of Mao Tse-tung himself, the proletarian nature has no preestablished social or even political organizational bearer. It is the proletarian values themselves as interpreted by Mao which will form the "proletarian revolutionary" elite. This elite will be drawn from all those human elements (Red Guards, PLA, and "good" cadres) who have demonstrated their proletarian revolutionary virtue.[14]

It might be urged that this apparent devaluation of the concept of the party marks a final qualitative break with the whole Marxist-Leninist tradition in which the concept of the party as the bearer of proletarian virtue is itself the holy of holies. It might be further urged that if the term "proletarian dictatorship" now refers to a syndrome of qualities and virtues (selflessness, submersion in the collectivity, uncompromising hatred of the enemy, renunciation of privileges and personal career interests, and lack of interest in material goods),[15] and if the word "bourgeoisie"

[13] The Chinese government has, to be sure, given a real weight to negative class background, however defined, but "positive" class background has never been taken as prima facie proof of the presence of virtue.

[14] It would appear that this notion has led some young enthusiasts to attack any institutionalization whatsoever of "revolutionary authority" and led them to see "bourgeois" corruption even in the newly formed "Revolutionary Committees." This "anarchist" deviation is now under severe attack.

[15] To Marx and even to Lenin the proletarian dictatorship was a prelude to the good society and not the good society itself. The proletariat possessed those virtues appropriate to the revolution, but not

refers to the corresponding vices, one could easily find a new, more naturally Chinese vocabulary to describe this historic moral conflict.

It is, however, precisely these Marxist-Leninist terms which seem to establish the links between Maoism and a universal (not specifically Chinese!) world-historic movement running back to the October Revolution and before that to Marx. It is precisely this sense of participation in a world historic drama transcending China which Mao himself is bent on preserving. One might, of course, ask why a new universal world historic movement, another "purer" Communism, might not originate de novo in China. Marxism-Leninism did not originate in a cultural limbo. It is a hybrid West European-Russian product. One might argue that it is as "culture-bound" as anything that might come out of China. Yet quite apart from Mao Tse-tung's own subjective convictions, there is probably an obscure realization on his part that no movement with a purely Chinese stamp could establish its universal claims in the whole non-Western world. The name of Karl Marx still carries an aura of universality which none of the non-Western intelligentsias or political elites are likely to concede to each other. Africans are not likely to accept the universal claims of a purely Chinese revolution any more than the Chinese are likely to accept "Arab socialism." Hence Mao's aspirations to leadership in a new world revolution are still inextricably tied—doubtless even in his own mind—to a world historic movement which did not originate in China. One might add that even vis-à-vis his own people he presents himself not merely as the leader of the Chinese people, but as the representative of a transnational historic force.

---

necessarily appropriate to the ultimate good society when it would have "annulled" itself along with all other social classes. In Mao's vision the proletarian virtues themselves are the virtues of the good society. They are not interim transitional values but ultimate values.

If Mao has not been able—and probably has not desired —to extricate himself from something called the Marxist-Leninist Communist movement, this means that Chinese behavior continues to affect the "World Communist Movement" (whatever it may be at present), and, conversely, the evolution of the Marxist-Leninist movement must continue to affect Chinese aspirations to establish Peking as the center of a recrudescent world Communist movement. China and the Soviet Union remain entangled with each other. The Chinese insistence that Soviet universal claims have now become a mask in the service of Soviet great power chauvinism simply raises the common suspicion that this may be no less true of China. Having played a central role in bringing about the disintegration of Communist authority in Moscow, Peking will find it difficult to reconstitute it for itself.

The notion frequently accepted abroad that Peking has become the bastion of Marxist-Leninist "orthodoxy" while Moscow has gone astray will simply not bear examination. Implicit in Mao's Cultural Revolution are theses which strike at the very heart of Communist assumptions hitherto widely accepted. We are now told that forty years of "socialism"—of the absence of private ownership of the means of production—have done nothing to prevent the "bourgeois" degeneration of Soviet youth. We are told that a ruling class the basis of whose power is clearly political and bureaucratic has become a "new class" and that Communist parties as such may become vehicles of "bourgeois dictatorship."

It is, of course, entirely likely that there will be a retreat in China from these more extreme Cultural Revolutionary theses to a more conventional version of Maoism.[16] It is

[16] Even as this is being written there are indications of a reluctant compromise by the Maoist group with resistant forces. How far the compromise will go is still far from clear.

particularly difficult to believe that the displacement of the party from its position of sanctity is compatible with the effort to create Peking-oriented groupings throughout the world (the Albanians, who are Peking's only truly faithful adherents, are still profoundly devoted to the mystique of the party). It is nevertheless difficult to believe that some of the questions raised by the Cultural Revolution will not leave a sediment of troublesome doubts in the minds of all. How these questions and doubts are likely to affect the future course of Chinese development we cannot know, but the relationship between Communism and China remains in flux.

In fact, the entire history of the People's Republic since 1949 has been one of enormous shifts and unanticipated changes. This does not mean that certain institutions and institutional habits have not taken root. It does not mean that there have not been solid and probably irreversible accomplishments, or certain constant patterns of behavior in some areas. It does mean that there has not yet emerged a complete, crystallized sociopolitical order nor even a complete, crystallized system of official beliefs.[17] The cultural crisis which has shaken China since the beginning of the century remains unresolved.

Many factors, both "objective" and "subjective," help account for this protean development. Peking's involvement with the evolution of Marxist-Leninist Communism has certainly been one of them. Far from being a factor of stability, the involvement with this world movement has been a factor making for convulsion and change. While elsewhere the crisis of Communism has led to "pragmatic" adjustments whose ulterior development we can hardly predict, in China it has led the aging Mao to project a new

17 There has been no equivalent of that whole Stalinist development between the early twenties and the fifties which made it possible for experts to delineate all the fixed features of the "Soviet system."

ecumenical vision of the good society. In a sense, it is still his image of himself as a Marxist-Leninist leader in the apostolic succession (and not his image of himself as a Chinese emperor) which encourages him to project this vision, but the vision itself has involved as ruthless a manhandling of the ideological fabric as the "pragmatism" of the Soviets and East Europeans. The terrible simplicity of the vision and the massive resistance to it suggests that it will not prevail in its more extreme form either at home or abroad. Yet even if Mao is succeeded by leadership which professes a more sober and modified "Maoism," China is still likely to move into an uncharted future not prefigured in the writings of Marx, Lenin, or Mao. The crisis of world Communism is also the crisis of Chinese Communism.

1

CHINA AND THE SOVIET THEORY OF "PEOPLE'S DEMOCRACY" (1954)

Introduction. The Soviet theory of "people's democracy" in all its developments and elaborations is the main addition to the "storehouse of Marxism-Leninism" since the end of World War II. Its application to the satellite states of Eastern Europe has been discussed in various places.[1] To the writer's knowledge, however, the Soviet effort to force Communist China into the category of "people's democracy" is a subject which has so far received little consideration.

It should be stated at the very outset that our interest here does not lie in theory as a determinant of action. It is quite possible to believe that there are core elements of the Marxist-Leninist tradition which do indeed shape patterns of behavior, without believing for a moment that the sort

NOTE: This essay was first published in 1954 as a pamphlet under the same title by the Center for International Studies, Massachusetts Institute of Technology, Cambridge, Massachusetts.

1 A good short account can be found in Gordon Skilling's "People's Democracy in Soviet Theory," *Soviet Studies,* nos. 6, 7.

of thing represented by the theory of people's democracy forms such an element. Like "the democratic dictatorship of workers and peasants," "the new democracy," and other such formulae, "people's democracy" represents a Marxist-Leninist sociohistoric analysis of the situation in a given period within a given area. On the whole, one finds that, if one assumes that such formulae reflect events and political policies, much more can be explained than if one assumes that the process is reversed. As a matter of fact, these formulae are often misleading even as a reflection of actualities. Communists often stress differences in theory which correspond to no differences in reality, and will subsume really different phenomena under the same theoretical category. To cite an instance, we shall have to draw a sharp distinction in this paper between the concept of "dictatorship of the proletariat" and China's "proletarian hegemony within a coalition of classes." Yet it is most doubtful whether this sharply drawn theoretical distinction corresponds to any actual difference in the internal power of the CCP and of the Communist parties of Eastern Europe and the Soviet Union.

Why, then, should we concern ourselves with these scholastic formulae? Because the manipulation of these formulae, the choice of one rather than another, furnishes us with one of the few indices we have—unsatisfactory as it may be—to political intent and to tensions within the Communist world; for, even when these formulae do not reflect the realities to which they presumably refer, they may nevertheless reflect concerns on other matters. Thus, while the stress on the difference between "dictatorship of the proletariat" and "proletarian hegemony" may not reflect any differences in the actual internal power of the CCP and the CPSU, it may nevertheless reflect certain significant aspects of Sino-Soviet relations.

"People's Democracy," 1944–1949. Before turning our attention to China, we must consider the evolution of the people's democracy concept, as applied to Eastern Europe. While the satellite regimes of Eastern Europe actually began to take shape in 1944 and 1945, it was not until 1947 that the famous academicians Varga and Trainin first undertook to fit these developments into a theoretical framework.[2] The main novel features which Varga enumerates are: (1) the fact that in Eastern Europe there are states under "proletarian hegemony" (that is, domination) which are not dictatorships of the proletariat, since parties representing other classes—the peasantry, the bourgeoisie, and the petty bourgeoisie—participate in the government; (2) the fact that there are states under "proletarian hegemony" in which the form of state is not of the Soviet type. It is these political features rather than such economic features as private property in land and the existence of a sector of private industry and commerce which mark off these states from the Soviet Union, because the Soviet Union had itself passed through a stage of private property in land and of private industry and commerce during the N.E.P. period. Varga even goes so far as to maintain that "a parliamentary democracy of the western type may well prove to be a viable form of government for these states, since in Eastern Europe the leading role of the Communist parties makes it certain that these governments will serve the people rather than the monopolistic bourgeoisie."[3] In seeking the causes of this novel development in Eastern Europe, Varga points to the existence of "feudal vestiges" which make it possible for the bourgeoisie to merge itself temporarily with "pro-

[2] See Varga's article, "Democracy of a New Type," *Mirovoe Khoziaistvo i Mirovaya Politika,* no. 3, 1947; and Trainin's "Democracy of a Special Type," *Sovetskoe Gosudarstvo i Pravo,* no. 1, 1947.

[3] "Democracy of a New Type," p. 6.

49

gressive" classes in the struggle against feudal landowners. (He overlooks the fact that Russia was not a whit less "feudal" than Poland or Rumania when Lenin proclaimed a "dictatorship of the proletariat." The fact that the old feudal classes were discredited in a common fight against the common aggressor, Nazi Germany, has cemented still further the amity among progressive classes.

When one seeks the actual reasons for this "novel" development of Eastern Europe, other factors come to mind. During the period between 1944 and 1947 the Soviet Union was still most anxious to hide from its erstwhile allies the true bases of power in Eastern Europe. This could certainly not be done by announcing "dictatorships of the proletariat" and by setting up soviets. Furthermore, in many of these countries the Communist parties had been most insignificant. To have immediately proclaimed the existence of a "dictatorship of the proletariat" would have deprived the party of the opportunity to capture and control other political organizations with deeper indigenous roots. It would have revealed in a glaring fashion the extent to which the political power of the Communist parties rested on Soviet bayonets rather than on local support. After the Tito crisis, Soviet theory was inclined to stress the role of the Red Army in making possible the "people's democracies" of Eastern Europe. During the period under consideration, however, there was more of a tendency to stress the historic, organic roots of these new regimes. Such may have been among the actual considerations leading to the shaping of the satellite regimes. Varga's use of the phrases "democracy of a new type" and "new democracy" leads to the speculation that, at this particular point, Soviet theoreticians may have been paying some attention to Mao Tsetung's "theoretical contribution" to the storehouse of Marxism-Leninism. There is, indeed, a strong resemblance between Varga's "democracy of a new type" and Mao's "new democracy." We have in both the concept of a particular type of "transition period based on a coalition of classes under proletarian hegemony"; land redistribution as a "bourgeois democratic" measure playing a large role; and "feudal vestiges" and the foreign enemy (or foreign imperialism) as a force uniting the "progressive" bourgeoisie to the other classes. And yet, if he was influenced by Mao, Varga nowhere acknowledges it. At one point, he mentions the experience of Outer Mongolia as a possible prototype of "democracy of a new type," but nowhere does he mention the "liberated areas" of North China. Neither at this time nor later do we find any acknowledgment of Mao's professed theoretical innovations in these matters. When we turn to Trainin, as a matter of fact, we find that he deliberately avoids the use of the word "new" in discussing the East European experience. Instead he uses the phrase "democracy of a special type" and "people's democracy"— the phrase which is to become official. Trainin's political instincts are sounder here than those of Varga (who often manages to embroil himself). To suggest the possibility of new developments not previsioned in Lenin's and Stalin's formulation before Stalin had himself proclaimed such novelties was a most risky procedure at best.

People's democracy is, of course, a "transitional stage" between capitalism and socialism, containing as it does a mixture of both "socialist" (state-controlled industry) and capitalist sectors. Varga and Trainin, however, do not discuss the whole problem of how people's democracy will "grow over" into socialism. They concern themselves exclusively with the past and the present. The future is left hanging in mid-air. It was precisely this studied vagueness in official Soviet theory concerning the "path to socialism" which made it possible for the more independent elements among the Communist parties of Eastern Europe to develop notions of "separate paths" of development for their

51

own countries—that is, paths which would diverge from the particular Soviet path to "socialism." The possibility was contemplated by some (Gomulka, for instance) that these states might be able to proceed to "socialism" (that is, a totally state-controlled economy on the Soviet model) without the fierce "class struggle" which marked the end of the N.E.P. in the Soviet Union; that such classes as the rich peasants and bourgeoisie might be "educated" into socialism; and so forth. Now there is no doubt that these people were self-convinced Communists, that is, thoroughgoing totalitarians. They were, however, reluctant to lose the broad base of control provided by the united fronts and coalition parties already under firm Communist control or, what is more important, to alienate the vast masses of the peasantry. Such may well have been the real considerations lying behind the talk of "separate paths" to socialism.

It is quite likely that a sharp reaction against talk of "separate paths" to socialism would have ultimately arisen in the Soviet Union even if no Tito crisis had occurred. Long before this, Stalin had tended to regard with suspicion any implication that the course of historic development of the Soviet Union "from capitalism to socialism" was not mandatory for the rest of the world (except in cases where Stalin himself had proclaimed the existence of peculiarities). Such opinions had been regarded before this as symptoms of organizational unreliability (for example, the conflict about the question of American "exceptionalism" in the early thirties). There can be no doubt, however, that the Tito crisis was the traumatic experience which immediately precipitated a sharp revision in the content of the theory of people's democracy. Ironically, as Adam Ulam points out in his *Titoism and the Cominform*,[4] Yugoslavia had probably sinned less than any of the other satellites in

[4] Cambridge, Mass.: Harvard University Press, 1952.

the matter of pursuing a "separate path" to socialism. Tito had been particularly zealous in his attempts to approximate the Soviet path. And yet to some extent, like the parties in all the other satellites, the Yugoslav party did occasionally speak of Yugoslavia's national peculiarities. Thus in seeking the presumed ideological roots of Tito's disgraceful behavior in resisting the undermining of his organization by Soviet subversion, it is not surprising that we find the Kremlin dwelling at great length on the sinister notion of the "separate path" to socialism. The drastic revision in the theory of people's democracy was announced by Dimitrov at the end of 1948 and later further developed by such Soviet theoreticians as Farberov, Mankovsky, and Yudin.[5] In brief, the new revisions clear up once and for all any doubts concerning what path the people's democracies will take towards socialism. There is only one way to socialism—the Soviet way. In the Soviet Union a "dictatorship of the proletariat" had been proclaimed during the October Revolution. Although economic concessions had been made during the N.E.P. period, they had been made under the auspices of the dictatorship of the proletariat, and it was only the dictatorship of the proletariat which had made possible the "building of socialism" during the period of the first five year plan. As for the people's democracies of Eastern Europe, they were already, in essence, dictatorships of the proletariat and were actually in their N.E.P. phase of development. In the words of Yudin, "State power in the countries of people's democracy fulfills the functions of the proletarian dictatorship." [6] Instead of concealing the complete domination of the Communist parties in these countries, this fact was now to be openly and stridently pro-

5 See, for example, Farberov's "New Moments in the Development of People's Democracy," *Sovetskoe Gosudarstvo i Pravo,* no. 5, 1949.

6 "The Lands of People's Democracy on the Way to Socialism," *Literaturnaya Gazeta,* May 1949.

claimed. Furthermore, just as the Soviet Union had achieved "socialism" only through a process of bitter "class struggle" against "bourgeois elements" and kulaks, so all the satellite states would have to pass through a stage of bitter class struggle if they were ever to reach the golden land of socialism. Tito—so it was claimed—had dared to hope that Yugoslavia could proceed to socialism hand in hand with all other elements in the Yugoslav "United Front."

No attempt was to be made, to be sure, to impose the Soviet state form on Eastern Europe. People's democratic states could fulfill the tasks of the proletarian dictatorships quite as effectively as the Soviet form. Here, it is interesting to note that, even in theory, the Soviets are now willing to admit the inconsequentiality of the question of the form of state (as opposed to the question of Communist party control). The revised theory of people's democracy also places tremendous emphasis on the "liberating" role of the Red Army.

When one inquires into the meaning of all this in terms of actual policy, one finds that the proclamation that "people's democracies" are in essence "dictatorships of the proletariat" simply makes official a state of affairs already existent—the supremacy of the communist parties in the satellite regimes of Eastern Europe. It does, however, symbolize the fact that henceforth the "Soviet path" would be mandatory. The promulgation of the necessity of "class struggle" did, however, really reflect the beginning of a drive toward collectivization, and a bitter campaign against the "bourgeoisie" and overly independent elements within the bosom of the party. This shift in theory does indeed correspond to some very crucial shifts in practice.

"People's Democracy" and China. Such, in brief, was the status of the theory of people's democracy when the Chi-

nese Communists achieved their spectacular victory in 1949. In the years since 1940, the Chinese Communists had presumably been operating within the framework of Mao Tse-tung's theory of "new democracy." As already indicated, this "new democracy" theory was in its main outlines very similar to the pre-1948 theory of people's democracy as expounded by Varga and Trainin. The main difference was the much greater emphasis on "feudal vestiges" and "imperialism" in Mao Tse-tung's formulation. Otherwise we find the same stress on the coalition of classes under proletarian hegemony, the same emphasis on the need to win the peasantry and retain the "national" ("progressive" in Eastern Europe) bourgeoisie, and the same insistence on the need for a mixed economy. On the question of the ultimate path to socialism, Mao Tse-tung is not too specific, but he does drop occasional suggestive hints. Thus, in the pamphlet "On Coalition Government" (1945), he strongly insists that China's path to socialism will be Chinese. "To the Russians," he states, "such a system [a pure "dictatorship of the proletariat"] is completely necessary and rational . . . Chinese history will create the Chinese system." [7]

Now the victory of Chinese Communism, welcome as it was, confronted the Kremlin with a problem on the ideological front. It had just succeeded in removing from the theory of people's democracy all elements which implied the possibility of a path of development differing from the Soviet path. How, then, was Mao Tse-tung's notion of "new democracy" to be related to the post-1948 conception of people's democracy? The Kremlin might, of course, have easily concluded that they were unrelated, that China as a "backward area" and semi-colony represented a development qualitatively different from the development in East-

[7] Conrad Brandt, Benjamin Schwartz, and John K. Fairbank, *A Documentary History of Chinese Communism* (Cambridge, Mass.: Harvard University Press, 1952), p. 305.

ern Europe. Stalin himself had, after all, previsioned and provided for the "peculiarities" of the Chinese development. During the period between 1949 and the day of Stalin's death, it became one of the main tasks of Russian experts on Chinese Communist history to stress the degree to which Stalin had provided for all the peculiar contingencies of Chinese history. Little room indeed was left for Mao's claims to have provided new creative insights. This, however, was all past history. Would China's path continue to be "peculiar" in the future?

Here we find that the strong antipathy which had developed in Moscow to all "peculiar paths" in general was to outweigh all other considerations. By the last months of 1949 we find articles in Soviet periodicals definitely categorizing China as a people's democracy. In the October 1949 issue of *Voprosy Ekonomiki* (no. 9) we find an article entitled "Problems of the National Colonial Peoples since the Second World War," by E. Zhukov, in which the following passage occurs: "People's democracy is a special form of regime which corresponds to the period of transition from capitalism to socialism. Its existence has been made possible by the victory of socialism in the U.S.S.R. and the strengthening of democratic forces throughout the world. It accords in full measure with the interests of the broad toiling masses of colonial and semi-colonial countries . . . It is capable of ensuring the liberation from imperialism and of realizing genuine democratic changes which will create the necessary conditions for the transition to socialism." There is, to be sure, a difference between people's democracy in the more highly developed countries of Eastern Europe and people's democracy in areas just emerging from colonialism and semi-colonialism. It is, however, a difference in degree of development—not a qualitative difference. "The range of bourgeois democratic tasks confronting people's democracy in these countries will be considerably greater than in other less backward, more developed areas which have not experienced, or virtually not experienced, the colonial yoke." Thus, within this context, Mao Tse-tung's "new democracy" simply represents a very primitive stage of people's democracy somewhat analogous to the 1944–1948 period of people's democracy in Eastern Europe. The inference to be drawn from this is obvious. However different, China's people's democratic development may have been in its earlier phases, in its latter phase there can be only one path of development for any people's democracy—the Soviet path. On its way to socialism, China must be transformed into a "dictatorship of the proletariat"; it must pass through a period of bitter "class struggle" against bourgeoisie and kulaks.

From 1949 until today [1954], this categorization of Communist China as a "people's democracy" with all its implied directives has become standard procedure in all Soviet writings on the subject. It should, of course, be added that this has by no means implied the application to Communist China of the actual policies being applied in Eastern Europe. If Titoism drove the Kremlin to drastic and ruthless efforts of suppression and *gleichschaltung* in those areas already under its effective control, in the case of Communist China it seems, on the whole, to have driven the Kremlin in the direction of caution and an unprecedented forbearance. This ideological measure rather seems to have been designed to place some sort of ideological constraint on China with regard to its future development. It served notice on the Chinese regime to eschew talk of "special paths" to socialism, to warn that the Soviet model in the "transitional stage to socialism" was absolutely mandatory and that any divergence from this model was a telltale sign of ideological weakness. At a time when the Kremlin itself was inclined to stress how relevant Mao's strategy for the seizure of power was to other lands of Asia, it pointed out

57

to other Asian Communist parties that only the Soviet Union provided the model for development once power had been seized. China might show Asia how to seize power. (There have since been reservations raised by Soviet writers concerning the "mechanical" applicability of the Chinese experience even on this score.) The Soviet Union alone could show it how to achieve socialism.

How, then, did the Chinese Communist hierarchy react to this categorization as a "people's democracy"? On the surface at least, we seem to note a degree of acquiescence. As early as July 2, 1949, we find that Mao Tse-tung's crucial speech of that date is entitled "On People's Democratic Dictatorship" rather than "On New Democratic Dictatorship"; and the "Common Program" presented to the People's Political Consultative Conference in June of the same year refers to the new state in China as "a new democratic or people's democratic state." Presumably the two terms are interchangeable. However, while the phrase itself receives some currency, a close examination of Mao's speech and of all other contexts in which the phrase is used makes it quite obvious that the post-1948 Soviet interpretation of the phrase has not been accepted. "People's democratic dictatorship" is something quite different from people's democracy. It is decidedly not a "dictatorship of the proletariat" but a dictatorship of the "people" (defined as being made up of four classes: proletariat, peasantry, petty bourgeoisie, and national bourgeoisie) operating under "proletarian hegemony." If this were all, it might be possible to maintain that "people's democratic dictatorship" is simply a primitive stage of "people's democracy." However, elsewhere within the same speech there are strong suggestions that the other classes of the "people" will be educated and reformed into socialism. "Only when there is a people's state, is it possible for the people to use democratic methods on a nationwide and all-round scale to educate and reform themselves, to free themselves from the influence of reactionaries at home and abroad . . . to un-learn the bad habits and ideas acquired from the old so-ciety and not to let themselves travel on the erroneous path pointed out by the reactionaries but to continue to advance and develop towards a Socialist and Communist Society." On the subject of the national bourgeoisie we find the following: "When socialism is realized, that is, when the nationalization of private enterprise has been carried out, they can be further educated and reformed. The people have in their hands a powerful state apparatus and are not afraid of the national bourgeoisie." [8] The per-spective of a "dictatorship of the proletariat" is nowhere mentioned.

There is thus a strong presumption that China's path to socialism will differ from the Soviet path and hence from the path of the people's democracies of Eastern Europe. This presumption is made even more explicit in certain detailed expositions of "new democracy" which have ap-peared in China since 1949. Thus Meng Hsien-chang in a book entitled *A Course on New Democratic Economy* (1951): "In general, new democratic states may be able to march toward socialism steadily without the necessity of another bloody revolution" (p. 175). He then cites the fol-lowing passage from a speech of Liu Shao-ch'i at the First Session of the People's Political Consultative Conference: "We need the revolutionary solidarity of our whole people not only to implement our new democracy but also to im-plement socialism." Another prominent theorist, Shen Chih-yüan, in a book entitled *The General Theory of New Democratic Economy* (1950) states: "The victory of new democracy in China and Southern and Eastern Europe has opened the prospect of a peaceful transformation to social-

[8] Brandt, Schwartz, and Fairbank, *Documentary History of Chinese Communism,* pp. 457, 458.

ism" (p. 7). It is curious to note here that, far fram bracketing China with people's democracy in the current Soviet interpretation, Shen brackets the East European development under the heading of new democracy as interpreted in China, thus blithely ignoring all the changes which had taken place since 1948.

Thus, while the phrase "people's democracy" is occasionally used to refer to China by the Chinese (although its use is highly infrequent as compared to "new democracy" and "people's democratic dictatorship") it is invariably defined in new democratic terms, for example, in Liu Shao-ch'i's speech of April 1951: "Our regime is a people's democratic regime—that is to say, in our state the people occupy the position of the head of the state. It is under the hegemony of the proletariat based on an alliance of peasants and workers."

When one turns from ideological definition to reality, of course one finds that the phrase "education and reform" when used in the totalitarian context may develop some very strange meanings. The so-called "Five-Anti" movement of 1952, directed against the national bourgeoisie, was carried on under the motto of "education and reform." To the businessmen who were forced into bankruptcy and hounded to death, the difference between "education and reform" and "elimination of the bourgeoisie as a class" may well have seemed somewhat pedantic. However, the fact remains that, whatever the real political and economic considerations lying behind this campaign, whatever its real consequences for private industry, it has actually led to no basic change on the ideological front. The national bourgeoisie is still one of the four classes of the people and may still be "educated and reformed" into socialism. The theoretical prospect of a Chinese path still remains.

Thus, at the time of Stalin's death the following state of affairs prevailed: (1) the Kremlin had definitely classed

Communist China with the people's democracies, and the inference was clear that, like other people's democracies, it could "build socialism" only after establishing a "dictatorship of the proletariat" and only through a process of bitter class struggle against bourgeoisie and kulaks (in the course of forced collectivization); and (2) the Chinese Communists were still clinging to their own conception of "new democracy" or "people's democratic dictatorship." When they used the phrase "people's democracy" they invariably interpreted it in terms of new democracy. The perspective was still that of a special Chinese path, which nevertheless leaned heavily on the "precious experience" of the Soviet Union. This path involved the possibility of "educating and reforming" the bourgeoisie and peasantry into socialism. The necessity of a "dictatorship of the proletariat" had not been mentioned.

Since Stalin's death, new factors have emerged on the scene in both China and the Soviet Union. For one thing, Communist China in 1953 announced the launching of its first five year plan. Now in the official, orthodox history of the Soviet Union, the inauguration of Stalin's first five year plan is marked by certain particular associations. It was supposed to have brought to an end the period of N.E.P. and marked the beginning of the "transition to socialism." By the time it was completed, socialism was presumably already in existence. China, however, has presumably not even reached the stage of N.E.P., since there is as yet no "dictatorship of the proletariat," and yet it is already proceeding to "build socialism." It is now becoming increasingly difficult for Soviet writers to pretend that China is still in a very primitive stage of people's democracy, since five year plans are not launched in primitive stages. There has, to be sure, been a tremendous emphasis in China of late on learning from the Soviet experience. The reading of certain chapters in Stalin's "History of the

61

CPSU" bearing on the N.E.P. and the first five year plan has been made obligatory for all cadres. It is customary to repeat that the "precious Soviet experience" is of "tremendous significance for China." Furthermore, there can be no doubt that in the field of actual practice Soviet planning techniques are being assiduously studied by the Chinese. Nevertheless, an editorial on the October Revolution appearing in *Jen-min Jih-pao* of November 7, 1953 ("The Light of the October Revolution is Illuminating our Forward Path") makes it clear that the Chinese experience will not be an exact replica of the Soviet: "The general line of development of our economy in the transition period represents a correct application to the concrete circumstances of our country of the theories of Lenin and Stalin on transition periods. Our general tasks are the realization of socialist state-controlled industrialization, the gradual advance toward cooperative development in agriculture and handicraft industries, and the implementation of reform in the sector of private industry and commerce . . . If we correctly apply the theories of Lenin and Stalin on transition periods to the concrete conditions of our country, we shall be able to lead China step by step toward socialism . . . Although many of the measures and methods adopted by our country during the transition period will differ in some respects from the N.E.P. of the Soviet Union, they have in common with the N.E.P. the aim of guaranteeing a constant forward advance of the national economy in order to lift the people's standards of living and cultural level." Thus the perspective of education and reform still exists, and there is still no mention of "dictatorship of the proletariat." Elsewhere we find such statements as the following: "Private economy will gradually be transformed into socialist economy by passing through various forms of state capitalism and other methods . . . The new democratic economy is our country's concrete mode of transition to a socialist economy discovered by Mao Tse-tung." [9] The promise of a role in the socialist economy is still being made to the "national bourgeoisie" so long as it behaves.

Now, while the discrepancies between Soviet and Chinese ideological developments on the subject of China are never openly discussed by Soviet or Chinese publications, a recent symposium by a group of "academic Stalinists" in a Japanese publication makes it amply clear that Communist theorists are not unaware of the existence of these problems. The phrase "academic Stalinists" is used here to refer to that large regiment of intellectuals in Japan thoroughly committed to Stalinism but apparently unaware of the demands of party discipline regarding the question of what subjects should or should not be discussed. The symposium appearing in the Japanese periodical *Keizai Hyōron* of November 1953 candidly raises questions such as the following: Is China already in its N.E.P. stage? If so, why is there no dictatorship of the proletariat? Can the transition to socialism in China take place under the aegis of a coalition regime if China is a people's democracy? Without entering into all the details of the discussion, it might be interesting to point out that, while some of the participants maintain that China will in the end have to undergo a "dictatorship of the proletariat" as a basic requirement of people's democracy, one of the participants vigorously denies that the launching of a five year plan means that China has reached the stage of "building socialism." None of the discrepancies are effectively resolved.

However, while these problems are being discussed by Stalinoid Japanese academicians, Soviet writings since the death of Stalin have on the whole tactfully refrained from discussing the ideological aspects of China's latest develop-

[9] "The Transitional Economy from Capitalism to Socialism," *Hsüeh-hsi*, no. 10, Oct. 1953.

ment. On the whole, Soviet articles on China's five year plan simply tend to dwell on the harmless questions of planning technology. This neglect of ideological questions, however, merely reflects a general tendency in all Soviet publication since Stalin's death toward a diminution of public discussion of ideological problems, whether it be a question of China, the Eastern Europe satellites, or the Soviet Union itself. One is here confronted with the following question: does this represent a fundamental change in the whole attitude toward the importance of ideological analyses, or is it simply a passing phase reflecting the political situation of the Soviet Union at the present moment? The present writer finds it difficult to believe that the leaders of the Kremlin would lightly cast off their role as infallible social engineers with an unfailing insight into the march of history at every point in time and space.

In the case of China, of course, the desire to placate the Chinese might be ample reason for not pressing embarrassing discussions at this point. However, while there has been little discussion of these problems, there has also been no reversal of the official Stalinist position. China is still invariably referred to as a "people's democracy," and no new interpretation of that concept has been forthcoming. Thus one may still assume, as of today, that, in the Kremlin view, there is only one path to socialism—the Soviet path.

On the other hand, as of today, the Chinese Communists, after making all due obeisance to Soviet experience, continue to resist the implications for China of the post-1948 Soviet interpretation of people's democracy. They continue to leave the strong presumption that there will be peculiarities in China's march to socialism. So long as they cling to this position, they can continue to maintain that "Mao Tse-tung's teachings" regarding the peculiarities of development in China (and the rest of Asia) have a relevance not only to the past but also to the future. They can continue to maintain that the Chinese development has a peculiar relevance for Asia, not only as a model for the seizure of power, but also as a model for the subsequent "transition to socialism."

2

COMMUNIST IDEOLOGY AND THE
SINO-SOVIET ALLIANCE (1957)

Few will quarrel with the notion that economic and power factors play an important role in Sino-Soviet relations. Many observers, however, tend to deprecate the role of ideology in shaping these relations. The assertion that ideology has played and will continue to play a leading role in this partnership is, of course, part of a larger assumption that ideology has played a significant role in the history of Communism in general. Since this proposition is rejected by many, any attempt to deal with the role of ideology in Sino-Soviet relations should be preceded by an expression of views on the larger question.

The Role of Ideology: Three Views. In the prolonged and complex discussion of this subject over the past decade, the outlines of three overriding points of view can be discerned,

NOTE: This essay was first published as Chapter 3 of *Moscow-Peking Axis: Strengths and Strains*, by Howard L. Boorman, Alexander Eckstein, Philip E. Mosely, and Benjamin I. Schwartz (New York: Harper & Brothers, for the Council on Foreign Relations, 1957).

at the risk of some oversimplification: the static ideological approach, the sociological approach, and the power approach. Perhaps no one view fits neatly into any of these three categories, and within the confines of each of these approaches there have arisen contending schools of thought. Nevertheless, the use of these categories is convenient for purposes of analysis. On the whole, all three approaches have been used to suggest the monolithic and unbreakable nature of the Sino-Soviet alliance.

The advocates of the static ideological approach tend to see in the history of Communism simply the implementation in practice of the ideas of Marx and Lenin. Lenin, Stalin, and Mao have simply carried into practice the blueprints of Karl Marx. Like the Communists themselves, those who uphold this approach are inclined to accept the view that Lenin, Stalin (at least until his recent denigration), and Mao have simply "extended and applied" Marx's teachings. For them, there is no problem of the relation of doctrine to practice. They may, to be sure, see in Lenin and Stalin the admixture of certain elements of Russian thought. In any case, however, the development of the Communist world is to be explained in terms of a monolithic Communist religion which directs and informs the actions of its leaders.

In their interpretation of Sino-Soviet relations, supporters of this approach simply point to the Communist religion, shared by the Chinese Communist and Soviet rulers. The common bonds of faith are sufficient to explain the present nature of the alliance and to insure its endurance in the future. Tensions of power, nationalism, differences in historic background, are all outweighed and will continue to be outweighed by the ideological bond. The facade of complete harmony which we find in official writings is to be taken at face value.

The advocates of the sociological approach may differ

67

among themselves in their accounts of the origins of Communist totalitarianism. Some of them may concede that ideology played some role in the beginning. Some of them may insist that the modern Russian social system (as well as the Chinese) is simply the projection into the present of the "oriental" society of the past, while some may explain Communism as the result of the confrontation of economically backward societies with the highly industrialized societies of the West. Whatever their differences on the question of genesis, they all tend to agree that Communist totalitarian society as "a going concern" is held together by iron relations of sociological interdependence and that the vicissitudes of ideology have little to do with the development of the system.

In explaining the evolution of Sino-Soviet relations, the advocates of the sociological approach tend to emphasize the growing basic similarities of social structure in the Soviet Union and in Communist China. They point to the role of the Communist Party in both societies, to the emergence of a ruling class of *apparatchiki* in both societies. They point to the totalitarian controls established in both societies and to the present appropriation by the Chinese Communists of the basic Stalinist model of economic development. Indeed at the present time the Chinese Communists seem more genuinely committed to the Stalinist pattern of economic development than even the more stalwart of the Eastern European satellites (although some hesitations and vacillations on this score were manifested at the Chinese Communist Party Congress in September 1956). In general, the sociological approach would insist that, to the extent that the social structures of China and the Soviet Union can be considered identical in all essential respects, the two states can be expected to work together for their common goals in world politics.

Advocates of the power approach emphasize the power

interests of ruling groups as the determining factor in both internal and external affairs. The totalitarian social system did not develop spontaneously or inevitably. Over the course of its history the Soviet leadership has confronted numerous situations to which it might have responded by courses of action different from those which it chose. However, the decisions of the ruling groups have been largely motivated by the desire to maximize and make secure their own power within the Communist world and in the world as a whole. All the decisions of the leaders can be explained in terms of the priority of power, and totalitarianism is the consequence of their highly successful efforts. Again, according to this view, the vicissitudes of ideology, as such, play no dynamic role in shaping the course of events.

In dealing with Sino-Soviet relations, some of the advocates of this approach are inclined to explain Sino-Soviet relations in terms of direct organizational control of the Chinese Communist government by the Kremlin. Those who reject this explanation and doubt the existence of direct control tend, of course, to stress the shared power interests of Communist China and the Soviet Union. It is not difficult to itemize a list of such common interests. Communist China and the Soviet Union probably share an interest in ejecting American influence from Asia in general, and from Japan in particular. They probably both desire to see Vietnam and Korea drawn completely into the Communist orbit. On the side of factors which tend to bind Peking to Moscow, it has been urged by some that a relatively weak China cannot afford to be hostile to a powerful Soviet Union with which it shares an exposed border several thousand miles long. Finally, since Mao's promulgation of the policy of "leaning to one side," China has become increasingly dependent on the Soviet Union for economic and military support. All these power factors taken together are, from this point of view, sufficient to explain and predict the nature of the Sino-Soviet alliance.

I would suggest that while the ideological approach in its static form is untenable, the evolution of ideology has, in fact, played a crucial role in shaping events within the Communist world. It is possible to assert both that the general tendency has been toward the disintegration of Marxist-Leninist ideology and that ideology has continued to be of basic importance even in its process of disintegration. One may accept without reservation the contention that, ever since Lenin began to use Marxism as a "guide to action," whenever actual circumstances have contradicted some basic point of doctrine, the doctrine has either been discarded as being unessential or has passed over from the category of an operational concept to the status of an empty verbal formula while some new "theoretical analysis" has been spun to rationalize the situation. With Lenin, the notion that the inexorable forces of the mode of production would themselves lead the workers to emancipate themselves; that the economic situation of the workers would directly create in them a proper socialist mentality; that capitalism would collapse at its highest point of development; that the bourgeois revolution would be led by the bourgeoisie—all these commonly accepted Marxist notions were simply discarded when they ran athwart the exigencies of current political demands. Lenin was, of course, extremely resourceful in devising new "theoretical analyses" to account for these and other shifts. Later, when the notion that a socialist revolution in backward Russia must be accompanied by a proletarian revolution in the West had ceased to have operational consequences, the theory of "socialism in one country" was devised to plaster over this decay in doctrine.

In spite of this steady decay, elements of ideology have continued to shape the Communist world in complex and subtle ways, and on many levels. If it is, indeed, a fact that the ideology has been disintegrating, this is in itself a fact of enormous consequences. The image which leaps to mind is that of a retreating glacier flowing into the sea. Huge chunks of the glacier fall off. The glacier, however, continues to flow and to shape the terrain over which it flows. The fact that the ideology is disintegrating does not preclude the possibility that residual elements of ideology continue to shape the world image of Communist ruling groups. It does not mean that these groups are indifferent to the process of decay or can ever afford to be indifferent even from the point of view of the power which they exercise or claim.

One of the difficulties is that the term "an ideology" suggests an organic, synthetic whole. Before it underwent its Leninist transformation, Marxism did, indeed, constitute a grandiose, albeit unstable, synthesis of nineteenth-century strands of thought. As Professor Gerschenkron states the dilemma, "it is tempting to suggest that in a very real sense the advent of the Bolsheviks to power spelled the end of Marxist ideology." [1] If he simply means that Marxism as an architectonic structure was destroyed, one might be inclined to agree. If he means that elements and combinations of elements drawn from the Marxist-Leninist complex of ideas have not continued to shape the Communist world, this would seem to be a serious oversimplification. After all, in the course of his own manipulations of doctrine, Lenin himself developed a derivative or secondary body of doctrine of his own, which subsequently came to form a part of the orthodoxy under the name of Leninism. Thus, in considering the role of ideology in the Communist world, it is by no means sufficient to compare the texts

[1] Ernest J. Simmons, ed., *Continuity and Change in Russian and Soviet Thought* (Cambridge, Mass.: Harvard University Press, 1955), p. 106.

of Marx with Soviet or Chinese realities. The mediating doctrines of Lenin must also be considered.

Even today elements of the Marxist-Leninist complex may still form part of the genuine belief-world of both the Soviet and Chinese Communist ruling groups. It is entirely conceivable that they still believe that in some fashion "History" is inevitably on their side; that in some fashion they ultimately embody the interests of the masses of mankind, because their power is based on a "socialized" economy; that "capitalism"[2] is doomed to destruction; and so forth. There is, of course, nothing in such beliefs which would contradict the power interest of these groups. On the contrary, such beliefs would add energy and *élan* to their power aspirations.

Leaving aside, however, the treacherous question concerning the subjective beliefs of the leaders, there still remains the question of the role of ideology within the power complex itself.

Thus, in studying the Communist Party as a political organism, it is possible to conceive of the party in the abstract as a sort of power machine which can operate independently of the state of mind of those who participate in it. Once one begins to study the party in the concrete, however, one speedily discovers that ideas concerning the cosmic role of the party, the relations of the party member to his party, and the "ideal" Communist Party member are the warp and woof of the party's very existence. If these ideas begin to fade, the leaders have every reason to be concerned.

The pursuit of power takes place continuously within the framework of the ideological tradition. Even if Stalin

2 Until recently, the entire non-Communist world was subsumed under this heading. Now, with efforts to woo non-Communist neutrals, these states are no longer shoved under the category of "world capitalism."

had not conceived of himself as a great Marxist-Leninist philosopher, the mere circumstance that he came to occupy Lenin's throne forced him to play the role of philosopher-king. The same holds true of Mao Tse-tung. Since Stalin's death, there has, to be sure, been a striking diminution in the attention devoted to ideological statements, but his successors have nevertheless been forced to place themselves on record concerning fundamental ideological issues. The very tendency of Khrushchev and his colleagues to treat ideological matters in a somewhat cavalier spirit is a factor which has had far-reaching consequences.

One enormously important aspect of ideology lies in the appeal which its symbols and moral claims exert on many elements in the non-Communist world, particularly in Asia. The Leninist theory of imperialism, the notion that the Communist Party represents the interests of the masses of mankind, the simplified Marxist-Leninist account of the progress of mankind, have had an immense appeal throughout the non-Western world, and the Soviet leadership has been able to exploit the widespread receptivity to these ideas in order to advance their own cause. Here, the ideological factor is simultaneously an immense factor of power.

Finally, it is by dint of its unique ideology that the Communist leadership has till now been able to claim that an unbridgeable abyss separates the "camp of socialism" from the unredeemed world. At least until the Twentieth Congress of the Communist Party of the Soviet Union, this notion of monolithic Communist solidarity involved much more than a mere commitment to something called "socialism." It involved the assertion that Marxism-Leninism as interpreted in Moscow provided the only authentic guide along the "path to socialism" and that the Soviet Union provided the only authentic model of socialism. Since the Twentieth Congress, to which we shall return later, some

73

striking new breaches have appeared. Here it was openly proclaimed that there are "many paths to socialism," even though the important reservation was made that socialism can be achieved only where Communist parties ("the working class and its vanguard" in Khrushchev's terms) hold the leading positions. The full extent to which this retreat in doctrine may have weakened the usefulness of ideology as an instrument for dividing off the world of darkness from the world of light is only gradually becoming apparent.

With Lenin and Stalin, ideology demanded not simply a commitment by all Communists to the "general truths of Marxism-Leninism" but also the unquestioning acceptance of Moscow's party line at any time and on any matter whatsoever. This strict commitment was, of course, based on the idea that the party, as the concentrated embodiment of the proletariat, had an unfailing grasp of the historic truth at any point in time. While, undoubtedly, one of Stalin's main obsessions was organizational control —the placing of his "own men" in all key positions of power—one unfailing criterion for measuring the loyalty of "his" men was their eager willingness to accept his ideological authority on all matters at all times and without question.

Stalin's image of a "socialist world" was one in which both organizational and ideological control would be centered in Moscow. In his mind, the two elements probably constituted two facets of a single whole. Any crack in one facet was bound to be reflected in a crack in the other. Thus, while Moscow's rupture with Tito may have arisen out of an issue of power, we need not assume any lack of serious intent when the Kremlin immediately began to seek out all sorts of defects in the Yugoslav Communist approach to ideology and to apply a more rigid ideological control to its satellites. The events of late 1956 in Poland

and Hungary, as well as the reaction of the ruling group in Moscow to these events, suggest that Stalin's successors have tended to believe that they could maintain organizational control even while partially relaxing ideological control. To Stalin, on the other hand, absolute ideological control was itself an essential component of power.

In sum, despite the general drift toward disintegration, ideology has continued to play a role as a part both of the genuine belief-world of the Communist leaders and of the power system itself. Its decay cannot but affect the strength of the power system.

Ideology has played and continues to play a crucial role in Sino-Soviet relations. The monistic ideological approach correctly stresses the importance of ideology, but it errs in its failure to perceive the stresses and strains which shape the evolution of the ideology. It completely overlooks the problem of the disintegration of ideology and the ways in which ideology is bent and strained when it encounters new and recalcitrant situations or when it becomes enmeshed with power interests. The monistic ideological approach would never have conceived of the possibility of anything like the Kremlin-Tito conflict.

On the other hand, the sociological approach to the problem of Sino-Soviet relations assumes that the mere existence in different states of identities in social structure will inevitably lead to indestructible alliances between them. The whole of human history argues against any such supposition; even within the bounds of Communist history, the Tito conflict is a case in point. Before 1948, Yugoslavia was creating a Soviet type of social structure at a faster pace and with more *élan* than any other state within the Communist orbit. When a conflict arose in the power sphere, however, the growing similarity of social structure proved to be of no consequence.

It is, furthermore, by no means easy to distinguish sociological from ideological facts. The role of the Communist Party in the Chinese system, the appropriation by the Chinese of the Stalinist model of economic development, have their ideological roots. The Communist Party as a political organization cannot be divorced from the whole ideological context within which the party operates. Of course, the Stalinist model of economic development might, conceivably, be adopted in some country without accepting the whole Marxist-Leninist ideology, as simply one model of economic development. In the case of China, however, the unquestioning acceptance of the Stalinist economic model was preceded by the prior acceptance of Marxism-Leninism. Most of the first-line leaders of the Chinese Communist Party had become Communists in the early 1920's before the Stalinist model had been crystallized in the Soviet Union. The "social basis" of their power, to be sure, is now very similar to that of the Soviet *apparatchik* class. This social fact, however, rests upon a prior commitment to a common ideology.

In considering the power approach to Sino-Soviet relations, it seems to me that we can reject at the outset the notion that Communist China is organizationally controlled from Moscow. The balance of evidence available indicates strongly that the alliance between Moscow and Peking is an alliance between two autonomous centers of power.

If we proceed to explain the alliance wholly in terms of common power interests, the results are inconclusive. We have listed above certain items which would argue for a meeting of interests. One can also enumerate possible points of friction. The question of the control of border areas—Turkestan, Outer Mongolia, Manchuria—offers one possible area of friction. The question of the relative role of the Soviet Union and China in non-Communist Asia is another. The trip of Khrushchev and Bulganin to South and Southeast Asia in 1955 was clearly designed to "sell" the Soviet Union in this area and hardly attests to any eagerness to see these areas pass completely into the Chinese orbit. It has been suggested by Alexander Eckstein that the economic alliance between the Soviet Union and Communist China is by no means a "natural" economic relationship, based on an inherent complementarity between the two economic systems.

The fact that a relatively weak China shares a common border with a strong Soviet Union would perhaps discourage any policy of open hostility, but there is a long distance between a policy of nonhostility and the close alliance which has existed since 1950 between these two powers. Under ordinary circumstances, a state in this situation might be expected to maintain a posture of correct relations with its neighbor while striving to checkmate its power by seeking strong allies elsewhere. In China's situation, this would correspond to the hoary tradition of using "the far-off barbarians to control the barbarians close at hand."

Of course, Communist China is now dependent on the Soviet Union for military, economic, and technical aid, but this one-sided dependence has resulted from a prior decision to "lean to one side." If Communist China were determined to break out of this form of dependence, it could probably do so, and, as a matter of fact, there is considerable evidence that at the present time the Chinese would be only too happy to reduce their peculiar dependence on the Soviet Union.

Neither sociological nor power factors can account fully for the peculiar alliance between the Soviet Union and Communist China. The factor of shared ideology, a shared core of belief, remains crucial. There are aspects of the alliance which can be explained only in terms of the overriding importance of this factor. The strenuous effort on the part of the Chinese Communists to make every detail of Soviet ideology available to the Chinese public is perhaps without parallel in the history of relations between states. The Chinese Communist leadership probably shares implicitly with the Soviet leaders the belief that "History" is on their side, that "capitalism" is doomed, that the Soviet model of industrial development represents "socialism," that Communist parties (although not necessarily the Soviet party alone) are the infallible instruments of history. There can be no doubt that they share the Soviet leaders' solicitude for strengthening ideology as an element of power.

The ideological aspect of Sino-Soviet relations has been a crucial, but also a highly problematic aspect, one which has been subject to numerous stresses and strains. Ideology has played a dynamic role, and yet has been constantly corroded by new historic circumstances and new power considerations.

Ideological Issues in Sino-Soviet Relations. Before 1927, the ideological development of Chinese Communism was inextricably enmeshed in the ideological conflicts which were then raging in the Kremlin.[3] The Chinese situation created problems which, in turn, provided grist for the mills of the various factions in Moscow, but in these conflicts the Chinese Communists themselves played a relatively passive role.

Between 1927 and 1935, it gradually became apparent that the Maoist strategy provided the only possible path for the growth of Chinese Communism. Although "Maoism" represented, in the first instance, a development in the area of strategy rather than ideology and, at that time,

[3] For a fuller account of ideological issues in Sino-Soviet relations during the period before 1937, see my *Chinese Communism and the Rise of Mao* (Cambridge, Mass.: Harvard University Press, 1951).

the Chinese Communists did not adopt any explicit party line differing from the formulas then dominant in Moscow, this new strategy had certain immediate implications for ideology. The isolation of the Chinese Communist Party from the industrial proletariat and its complete dependence on peasant support for its survival struck directly at the notion that a Communist party must have some visible tie to the urban proletariat which it claims to represent. In all of Lenin's writings, as well as in Stalin's *Problems of Leninism,* the necessity for the link with the proletariat was taken for granted. It is, of course, quite true that Lenin's concept of a self-directed party and Stalin's actions in practice had opened the door to the divorce of the party from the proletariat, but nothing in their own experience had forced them to discard this element of Marxist orthodoxy.

Until the early 1930's, the notion that a Communist party must secure for itself an industrial proletarian base still had operational consequences, as is clear from the Kremlin's nagging directives of that time to the Chinese party. Again, this does not mean that Stalin was concerned only with maintaining the purity of an ideology. As always, he was obsessed with the problem of placing his own trusted men in key positions of power. It is no accident, however, that those whom he regarded as his men (first, Li Li-san, later, Wang Ming and others) shared his views on the necessity of urban proletarian support. While political considerations may in the end always override considerations of ideological purity, it is wrong to assume that Stalin ever abandoned ideological positions in a spirit of cavalier nonchalance. Every abandonment of an ideological position weakened to some extent the fabric of the ideology as a whole, and ideology itself was a crucial element in the whole power complex.

With the clear emergence of the Maoist strategy as the

only viable path in China, the notion of the necessity of an actual urban proletarian base ceased to have operational consequences. This element of orthodoxy had become a dead letter. The Chinese Communists have, as a matter of fact, even boasted of this peculiar development of Chinese Communism as one of Mao Tse-tung's unique contributions to the storehouse of Marxism-Leninism. Mao has demonstrated, as it were, that a party guided by a correct Marxist-Leninist philosophy can convert intellectuals and peasants into spiritual proletarians. The party's proletarian essence is no longer guaranteed by maintaining ties to its supposed class base but wholly by its possession of the correct proletarian doctrine. The Chinese example shows how the corrosion of doctrine can take place not only in Moscow, but also in other sectors of the Communist world.

Another gap in the ideological relations of the Chinese and Soviet parties was not to become apparent until after the Chinese Communists had assumed power in 1949. This divergence arose over the problem of "people's democracy."

China and the Concept of "People's Democracy." The rise of the Chinese Communists to power followed hard on the heels of the crisis which had been touched off by the break with Tito. Mao's assumption of power in China may well have coincided with a certain disturbance in Stalin's image of a "socialist camp." As Adam Ulam has pointed out in *Titoism and the Cominform,*[4] previous experience had probably led Stalin to believe that a mere assertion of his displeasure, a mere verbal chastisement by the Kremlin, would be sufficient to undermine Tito's power. Subsequent events demonstrated that a Communist party which had created its own power base within a given nation, a party led by its own dynamic leader fully familiar with Communist techniques of control, could not easily be cap-

[4] Cambridge, Mass.: Harvard University Press, 1952.

tured from within once it had achieved state power. In the so-called people's democracies of Eastern Europe, which were already under effective Kremlin domination by 1948, this realization led to a tightening of both organizational and ideological control. In the case of China, where the party's history had been not unlike that of Yugoslavia, it led the Kremlin to display a new circumspection.

If Stalin's ultimate image of the "socialist camp" continued to be that of a world tightly controlled from the Kremlin, one may surmise that after 1949 he postponed, rather than renounced, his hope of ultimately gaining control of the Chinese Communist Party. Up to his death, he seems to have accepted, however reluctantly, the necessity in practice of treating the Chinese Communist regime as an autonomous center of power.

While not much could be done toward instituting organizational control over China, every effort was made to reassert the Kremlin's ideological supremacy. Every Soviet account written before Stalin's death of Chinese Communist history stressed again and again that all the theoretical foundations of the Chinese Communist victory had been laid by Stalin. Moscow made no concessions to Chinese claims that Mao had made original theoretical contributions to the storehouse of Marxism-Leninism. In all Soviet accounts, Mao figured, at most, as the talented executor of Stalin's theoretical teachings.

At the same time, every effort was made by Moscow to fit Communist China into the category of the "people's democracies" as that concept was interpreted after 1948.[5] This very effort disclosed an ideological gap between the two leaderships.

The concept of "people's democracy" was first elaborated

[5] For a fuller discussion of this question, see my article on "China and the Soviet Theory of People's Democracy," U.S. Information Agency, *Problems of Communism*, vol. 3, no. 5 (Washington: GPO, 1954), pp. 8–15.

as a theoretical framework to explain the nature of the So-
viet-imposed regimes of Eastern Europe. According to the
theory as it was developed before 1948, these regimes were
presumably coalition governments made up of bourgeois,
petty-bourgeois, peasant, and proletarian elements under
the "hegemony of the proletariat." While the notion of
united fronts under "proletarian hegemony" was not new
to Communist strategy, the peculiar feature of the new situation lay in the fact that united fronts now governed several states, and a new theory was required to account for
the difference between this new form of government and
the "Soviet" form. It was also necessary to explain why non-
Communist parties were included in these governments.
Another peculiar feature of these regimes was that they still
had many "bourgeois-democratic" tasks to perform before
reaching the stage of "socialist" development.

Before 1948 not much attention was devoted in the writings of theorists such as Varga and Trainin to the question
of the future development of these states. This prudent
reticence probably arose from a desire to stress the "united
front" aspects of the satellite regimes during their period of
initial consolidation. There were, however, spokesmen,
many spokesmen like Gomulka in Poland, who took advantage of this diffidence to hint that their own nations might
pursue "a path to socialism" differing somewhat from that
which had been followed by the Soviet Union.

After the break with Tito, Moscow announced clearly
and abruptly that there was only one road to socialism, the
Soviet road, and that all the "people's democracies" would
have to tread that path. The Soviet Union had been able to
make the transition from the quasi-capitalist stage of the
New Economic Policy to the socialist stage only because its
state was based on the "dictatorship of the proletariat." According to Lenin's dictum, while different countries might
display certain variations in their forms of government dur-

ing the period of transition to socialism, in essence all governments of this type would have to be dictatorships of the proletariat. After 1948 Moscow constantly reiterated that the regimes of Eastern Europe were, in their essence, dictatorships of the proletariat on the road to socialism and that they should behave accordingly. Again, in Stalin's mind, effective organizational control involved firm ideological control, and firm ideological control involved a total acceptance of the Soviet model of development. The whole Soviet development had, after all, been merely the "historic actualization" of the truths of Marxism-Leninism-Stalinism.

At this point, it will be useful to consider the theoretical difference between the "hegemony of the proletariat" and the "dictatorship of the proletariat" as expounded in the most recent edition (1952) of the Soviet *Encyclopaedia*. The definitions which it presents reflect the crystallized orthodoxy of the Stalin era, but they are also solidly based on pronouncements by Lenin. Basic to the difference between the two concepts is the entire notion of the two-stage development of noncapitalist countries, or of countries in which capitalism has been developed but feebly. On their path to socialism all these countries must pass through a "bourgeois-democratic" stage. During Russia's 1905 revolution, Lenin clung to the view that Russia was not yet ready for socialism and still had to traverse a period of "bourgeois-democratic" development. However, in Russia the bourgeois-democratic revolution would be carried out not by the weak and perfidious Russian bourgeoisie, but by the peasantry in alliance with the proletariat. The peasantry would represent the "bourgeois" element in this alliance, since its demands for land and political freedom were essentially bourgeois demands.

During the bourgeois-democratic stage, the proletariat would, of course, not be strong enough to establish its own exclusive class dictatorship, but would have to ally itself with other classes, notably the peasantry, which were interested in the overthrow of feudalism. It would have to circumscribe its program to conform to the "bourgeois" demands of its class-allis—demands for land distribution, civil rights, an effective parliament, and so forth. However, within this alliance, by dint of its historic destiny, the proletariat would gradually be able to achieve a position of "hegemony." The concept of the "hegemony of the proletariat" is defined in the *Encyclopaedia* as "the leadership of the toiling masses of city and countryside by the proletariat in the revolutionary struggle to carry to an end the bourgeois-democratic revolution, to establish a dictatorship of the proletariat, and to bring a Communist society into being."[6]

The concept of "dictatorship of the proletariat" becomes relevant only when the stage of transition to "socialism" is close at hand. In the words of the Encyclopaedia, "The dictatorship of the proletariat is the state power of the proletariat in the transitional period from capitalism to Communism, established as a result of the revolutionary overthrow of the power of the bourgeoisie and the smashing of the bourgeois state apparatus."[7] In defining the concept of dictatorship, Lenin states that "the scientific concept of dictatorship means nothing more nor less than unrestricted power absolutely unhampered by laws and regulations and resting directly on force."[8] Within a dictatorship of the proletariat, power is exercised exclusively by the proletariat and by its vanguard, the Communist Party, against all "exploiting classes," for the proletariat and the proletariat alone can achieve socialism. Both Lenin and Stalin stressed, of course, that the dictatorship of the prole-

---

[6] *Bol'shaia Sovetskaia Entsiklopediia,* 2nd ed. (1952), vol. 10, p. 311.
[7] *Ibid.,* vol. 14, p. 344.
[8] *Ibid.,* vol. 14, p. 342.

tariat represents not only the proletariat but the "numerous non-proletarian toilers, notably the 'rural proletariat.' " [9] It represents thus a "special form of alliance" in which only one of the allies possesses actual political power.

The *Encyclopaedia* emphasizes that the problem of the "dictatorship of the proletariat" constitutes "the main problem of Marxism-Leninism, for it is this concept which divides Lenin irrevocably from all social democrats."

Having decreed that the "people's democracies" were, in essence, "dictatorships of the proletariat," the Kremlin was not slow to extend this concept to the new developments in Asia. There were, to be sure, differences between North Korea, China, and Eastern Europe. Because of their backwardness, the Asian states of the "socialist camp" still had many "bourgeois-democratic" tasks to complete. However, once these states approached the period of the transition to socialism, they would necessarily become dictatorships of the proletariat.

It was precisely on this issue that a marked gap continued to exist between Chinese Communist and Soviet theory throughout the period from 1949 to the Twentieth Congress of the Communist Party of the Soviet Union in February 1956. While the Chinese were willing to accept the term of "people's democracy" as equivalent to their own "new democracy," they did not accept the post-1948 interpretation of this concept. In the interests of ideological harmony, the gap was not advertised. Nevertheless, it persisted and was even enshrined in the preamble to the Chinese Constitution of 1954.

As early as 1952, the Chinese Communists proclaimed the beginning of the period of transition to socialism, but they failed to acknowledge the necessity for a dictatorship of the proletariat in China. On the contrary, in China the party of

[9] *Ibid.*, vol. 14, p. 345.

the proletariat would proceed all the way to socialism in alliance with the peasantry, the petty bourgeoisie, and the national bourgeoisie under the "hegemony of the proletariat." The "bourgeois" sectors of the economy and even the minds of the bourgeoisie would be peacefully transformed, step by step, until they merged into socialism. During the last months of 1956, the Chinese Communists speeded up this "peaceful transformation." Private industry was converted into "state capitalist enterprises" at a greatly accelerated rate and the bulk of the "national bourgeoisie" were pictured as joyfully welcoming the new order, thanks to the intense "education" which they had undergone. The novel notion here is that an "exploiting class" may be "educated" into accepting socialism. It is interesting to note that not only has the facade of coalition government been maintained, but in recent months there has been a new propaganda emphasis on the participation of non-Communist "democratic groups" in this government, thus emphasizing the compatibility of such groups with "socialism."

This does not mean that the rich peasants and the "national bourgeoisie" have ceased to be exploiting classes in the Chinese interpretation of Communist ideology. So long as the bourgeoisie continues to exist as a class, it is an "exploiting" class and will go on exuding its noxious bourgeois ideology. However, the "hegemony of the proletariat" over the state makes it possible to contain the effects of this noxious influence. Meanwhile, an immense effort to "educate" these exploiting classes to the acceptance of socialism (the "Three-Anti" and "Five-Anti" movement of 1952 is interpreted as part of this educative process) has been under way. Some elements of these classes will prove uneducable, but the class as a whole will be peacefully transformed, and its members may even expect to hold honorable managerial positions in the new economy.

The authoritative *New China Monthly Gazette (Hsin Hua Yüeh Pao)* of October 1955 extolled this "different" Chinese path as constituting a new contribution to Marxist-Leninist theory. "One of Mao Tse-tung's brilliant contributions to the storehouse of Marxism is the principle that under certain sociohistoric conditions, in a state in which the proletariat has gained power, it can carry out a basic transformation of the capitalist elements in accordance with Socialist principles. None of the previous classics of Marxism-Leninism contain this type of theory, and no other state in the world has ever had this experience. In the Soviet Union and the people's democracies of Southern and Eastern Europe, capitalism is being eradicated by violent and forceful means. However, because of the concrete conditions of our country, we are able to arrive at the same goal—the eradication of capitalism—by peaceful methods of socialist transformation." [10]

The *New China Monthly Gazette* developed the notion that the Soviet Union had required a dictatorship of the proletariat because the Russian bourgeoisie had proved formidable and hostile in the revolution of 1917. The same was true of Eastern Europe. In China, however, the national bourgeoisie had been weak and tended to cooperate with the proletariat; hence, the possibility of a "peaceful transformation" of the bourgeois class. The concept of the "dictatorship of the proletariat" is here reduced from the status of a universal truth to that of a local Russian response to a parochial Russian situation.[11] It implies that in China the whole "people," and not the industrial proletariat alone, is "building socialism." There is a kind of straining toward the notion that the Communist Party is not

10 Shu Wei-k'ung, "The Gradual Tempo of China's Transitional Period."

11 It is interesting that Khrushchev took up this same idea at the Twentieth Party Congress of the CPSU.

merely the class party of the proletariat (although this is always mentioned), but somehow an embodiment of the "general will" of the Chinese nation as a whole, with the exception of those labeled as "counterrevolutionaries."

What, if any, have been the practical consequences of this ideological divergence? It may be reflected in certain features of the Chinese scene. The extraordinary emphasis on "ideological remolding" and on "persuasion" (in the Chinese sense), the genuine desire to make maximum use of the talents of the so-called "national bourgeoisie," the sedulous maintenance of the outward trappings of coalition government, the recent courting of the so-called democratic groups and parties, are all reflections of it.

On the other hand, whether the Chinese Communist Party calls its rule "hegemony of the proletariat" or "dictatorship of the proletariat," its effective control of China is not one whit less absolute than that of the Communist Party in the Soviet Union. While a facade of coalition government is maintained,[12] the so-called democratic parties echo the Communist Party line with parrot-like monotony. Furthermore, the Chinese seem to be implementing the Soviet model of economic development far more vigorously than any of the avowedly "proletarian dictatorships" of Eastern Europe.

The persistence with which the Chinese have clung to their "difference" may well have a significance above and beyond its implications for domestic policy. This persistence has maintained and magnified the image of Mao Tsetung as a great theoretical innovator in his own right. By the same token, it has reaffirmed the ideological autonomy of the Chinese Communists within the "socialist camp." Further, by stressing the "peculiarity" of China's path to

[12] The so-called democratic groups and parties, such as the Democratic League, the Revolutionary Kuomintang Committee, etc., are all represented in the governmental structure.

socialism—the ability of the Chinese Communists to march to socialism at the head of the "whole people"—Peking tacitly indicates to non-Communist Asia that China offers its peoples a uniquely relevant message, distinct from that of Russian Communism.

The Closing of the Gap. What has been the effect of Stalin's death on the ideological relations between Moscow and Peking?

Immediately after his death, there began, within Russia, a relatively cautious diminution of the Stalin image. With this, it became possible to drop the previous insistence on Stalin's decisive role as the theoretical engineer of the Chinese Communist victory. It immediately became possible to make some concessions to the claims made in China for Mao as a theoretical leader in his own right. Both before and after Stalin's death, Mao's writings were being translated into Russian and were reviewed extensively. While the reviewers conceded that Mao had "creatively" applied Marxism-Leninism to Chinese conditions, they did not go so far as to specify his concrete contributions to the "storehouse of Marxism-Leninism."

Considerable credit was now being given to Mao as the architect of the Chinese Communist victory, but the gap still remained between the Soviet concept of "people's democracy" and the Chinese interpretation. Although the years 1952–1955 were marked by a sharp diminution in Soviet discussions of ideology, whenever the issue was discussed, as in the 1954 party textbook on *Political Economy,* Moscow reaffirmed emphatically the standard dogma of the universal necessity for the dictatorship of the proletariat during the period of transition to socialism.

Strangely enough, during the last few months of 1955, on the very eve of the epoch-making Twentieth Party Congress, there was actually a revival of emphasis on this dogma. An article by K. Dubina, published in *Kommunist* (no. 15, October 1955), on "The Leninist Theory of Socialist Revolution," restated the Soviet position with renewed vehemence. "The experience of building socialism in the countries of the people's democracy," he wrote, "has clearly demonstrated the utter groundlessness of the chatter on the part of nationalist, opportunist elements who assert that their countries are proceeding to socialism by some special path, new in principle as it were and excluding class war, by the path of a peaceful growing over of capitalism into socialism." The universal necessity of the "dictatorship of the proletariat" was again stressed as the be-all-and-end-all of Communist orthodoxy.

Even more significantly, the same theme was developed by Kaganovich in his speech of November 6, 1955, celebrating the thirty-eighth anniversary of the October Revolution. At the very beginning of his speech Kaganovich proclaimed: "Only he is a Marxist, Lenin wrote, who extends the acceptance of the class struggle to the acceptance of the dictatorship of the proletariat. This is where the profound difference lies between a Marxist and an ordinary petty (and even big) bourgeois. This is the main thing in Marxism-Leninism and the fundamental thing in the October Revolution."

It is also interesting to note a rather peculiar use of Communist terminology in the slogans which *Pravda* published for the same anniversary of the revolution. One slogan conveyed Soviet greetings to the people's democracies, including such backward countries as Albania and Outer Mongolia, which are "constructing socialism." Another conveyed greetings to the Chinese People's Republic which is constructing "the foundations of socialism." Since the attacks of February 1955 on Molotov's much advertised error, there can be no misunderstanding of the profound difference in Soviet usage between "socialism" and "the foundations of socialism." Clearly, the distinction thus drawn between Albania and China did not lie in Albania's more advanced state of economic development but in the fact that China had not yet proclaimed itself a dictatorship of the proletariat.

The fact that these reassertions of orthodoxy were being pressed on the very eve of the Twentieth Party Congress, which was so soon to move in precisely the opposite direction, lends much weight to the hypothesis that deep differences of opinion on these ideological issues were being fought out in the highest policy-making circles. If Khrushchev and those close to him were then pressing for the adoption of the more elastic formulas which finally prevailed at the Twentieth Congress, it is conceivable that the more orthodox views expressed just prior to it reflected the vehement feelings of the opposition group, headed perhaps by Kaganovich. The sober and unenthusiastic tone of Kaganovich's speech at the Twentieth Congress would tend to reinforce this hypothesis.

An article in *Problems of Philosophy* entitled "How Do We Explain the Diversity of State Forms of Dictatorship of the Proletariat?" foreshadowed a new and more flexible approach.[13] After describing the peculiarities of Chinese Communist development, including the notion of the peaceful transformation of the bourgeoisie, the author then proceeded to accept this variant "path to socialism" as a legitimate subvariety of the "dictatorship of the proletariat."

The real turning point was the Twentieth Congress of the CPSU. Not only were the Chinese and Yugoslav paths to socialism declared fully legitimate, but Khrushchev himself went far beyond the Chinese in asserting "the possibility of employing the parliamentary form for the transition to socialism." This formulation, it is true, was by no means

13 I. A. Arkhipov, in *Voprosy Filosofii,* no. 6, Jan. 1955.

unambiguous. The notion that parliaments and united fronts might properly be utilized by Communist parties in their march to power is by no means an original one. What Khrushchev seemed to be suggesting, however, was that Communist parties operating in countries of "bourgeois democracy" could now legitimately claim that the achievement of socialism did not necessarily require "the smashing of the old state apparatus." The Soviet path to socialism, Khrushchev now states, was simply a Russian response to Russian conditions, to the intransigence of the Russian bourgeoisie at the time of the revolution.

The verbal formula "dictatorship of the proletariat" has not been dropped. It has simply been emptied of all semantic content. Moscow now proclaimed that Communist parties may use the "bourgeois" state apparatus to achieve socialism, that in some countries, as in China, socialism can be achieved by a multiclass coalition under "proletarian hegemony," and that, under some circumstances, the bourgeoisie may give up power without an armed struggle. To the extent that the term "dictatorship of the proletariat" had any meaning, it denied each of these possibilities. It is not strange that the Soviet leaders have been reluctant to drop the verbal formula. It was a concept which has played a central role in Marxist-Leninist ideology. As Kaganovich remarked, ". . . it had been the main thing in Marxism-Leninism."

Despite their assertion of the possibility of a variety of roads to socialism, Khrushchev and Co. have not left their ideological position entirely unprotected. While the paths to socialism may now vary, "the political leadership of the working class and its advance detachment is the indispensable and decisive factor for all forms of transition to socialism." In other words, socialism cannot be achieved except through the leadership of the Communist parties. What Khrushchev has been saying to those Communist parties which are not in power is, in effect, that the Soviet

Union is as interested as ever in having them attain power, but is no longer interested in the theoretical formulas and strategies which they may use to attain it. So far as both China and Yugoslavia are concerned, the new line, nevertheless, constitutes a striking admission of their claim to enjoy ideological autonomy, if not outright ideological independence.

In speculating on the pressures which lie behind these new revisions of doctrine, it would, of course, be one-sided to attribute them entirely to Moscow's need for closing the ideological gap with Communist China. The notion of the legitimacy of the parliamentary road to socialism was undoubtedly designed to improve the fortunes and freedom of maneuver of the French and Italian parties. The desire to win back Tito's allegiance to the "socialist camp" was undoubtedly another factor of immense importance in the doctrinal pronouncements of the Congress.

Events subsequent to the Twentieth Congress demonstrated that Moscow's hopes were premature, for important gaps still persisted between the ideological positions of the two parties. The Yugoslavs have, in fact, furnished a vivid example of how far the revision of ideology can be carried when Moscow no longer exercises any semblance of ideological control. The Yugoslavs have not only denied the necessity for instituting a dictatorship of the proletariat, but have even asserted that in some countries Social Democratic parties may become vehicles for the achievement of socialism, that many classes may participate in the building of socialism, and that even the forms of socialism may vary from country to country.[14] In this there is hardly a tenet of Marxism-Leninism which retains any absolute value. The

[14] For an exposition of these views, see, for instance, Jovan Djordjevic, "A Contribution to the Discussion of Social Classes and Political Parties," *Review of International Affairs* (Belgrade), vol. 6, no. 124 (June 1955), pp. 8–10; also R. Lowenthal, "New Phases in Moscow-Belgrade Relations," U.S. Information Agency, *Problems of Communism*, vol. 4, no. 6, pp. 1–10.

role of ideology as an instrument for drawing a firm qualitative distinction between the "camp of socialism" and the outside world is obliterated completely.

The Twentieth Congress by no means went the full way toward accepting these Titoist innovations. Evidently, Moscow's hope was that, if it went some way in meeting the Yugoslav's ideological demands, the latter would reciprocate by retracting their more drastic tamperings with the remaining fabric of the ideology. Its hopes have not been realized, and the Yugoslav Communists have not refrained from pressing their own views on the Soviet satellites in Eastern Europe. Whether the events of late 1956 in Poland and Hungary will make the Belgrade leadership more cautious or still more forthright in pressing for the recognition of not only "national" but independent paths to socialism remains to be seen.

Whatever Khrushchev's calculations as to the effects elsewhere of his revisions of dogma, the Kremlin's desire to close the ideological gap with Communist China was certainly of primary importance. Peking's assertion of China's unique path to socialism, in one sense, presented Moscow with a more pressing problem than did the case of Yugoslavia, precisely because China was in the "socialist camp," whereas Yugoslavia, by its own declaration, was not. At the Twentieth Congress, the Chinese case was mentioned repeatedly as an illustration of the "creative application of Marxism-Leninism." Shepilov, who became Foreign Minister three months later, dwelt in some detail on the peculiar features of the Chinese path and added, significantly, that "from the viewpoint of scholastics of Marxism, such an approach to the problem of transforming exploiting ownership into Socialist ownership is tantamount to trampling underfoot the principles of Marxism-Leninism; in actual fact this is creative Marxism-Leninism in action." [15] In dis-

15 The reference to the "scholastics of Marxism" suggests that the viewpoint attacked here actually had support in high party circles.

cussing the question of "paths to socialism," the Resolutions of the Twentieth Congress singled out China as the test case par excellence: "The Chinese People's Republic has introduced many special features into its form of Socialist construction. Before the victory of the revolution, the economy was extremely backward and was semi-feudal and semi-colonial in character. On the basis of its ability to capture the decisive commanding heights, the People's Democratic Government is now bringing about a peaceful transformation of private industry and commerce and their step-by-step conversion into component parts of socialism."

The Soviet leadership has conceded China's right to follow its own path to socialism, and it has thus closed the ideological gap, even though the verbal formula "dictatorship of the proletariat" has not been dropped. An indication that the Chinese Communists interpret the Congress' action in this light is furnished by the Chinese Politbureau statement of April 4, 1956, entitled "On the Historic Experience Concerning the Dictatorship of the Proletariat." While the main significance of this document is that it clarifies China's attitude toward the current denigration of Stalin, from the point of view of this paper, its main significance lies in the fact that for the first time in Chinese Communist history this document classifies China as a "dictatorship of the proletariat." It specifically equates China's "people's democratic dictatorship" with the dictatorship of the proletariat. Since the Soviets have now redefined this term in such a way as to remove all its meaning content, the Chinese are able to reciprocate by accepting the term, for in accepting it, they have conceded nothing of their own views concerning China's "peculiar path." The gap has been closed, not by bringing the Chinese ideological formula into line with Moscow's orthodoxy, but by adjusting Soviet ideology to accommodate the Chinese innovations. Ideological solidarity has, thereby, been reaffirmed.

The price, however, has been the reaffirmation of China's

ideological autonomy and a further tampering with what remains of Marxist-Leninist ideology. In the short run, ideological solidarity can, presumably, be maintained only through ideological concessions; in the long run, the weakening of the ideology as a coherent whole cannot but exercise a weakening effect. If the ideological link has been a crucial one in Sino-Soviet relations, the constant wearing away of the core of shared ideological beliefs must inevitably weaken that core, and the alliance must come to rest more and more on the shifting sands of power interest.

The Ideological Link: Will It Bind? A larger question emerges: What is the Kremlin's present conception of a Communist world? Have the Soviet leaders reconciled themselves to the vision of a Communist camp in which all Communist parties will enjoy both organizational and ideological autonomy, united only by a minimum core of shared beliefs?

The initial reaction of the Khrushchev leadership to the events of October and November 1956 in Poland and Hungary tended to indicate a confidence on their part that the ideological concessions which they had made to China and Yugoslavia were entirely compatible with maintaining their organizational control over the East European satellites.

The ruthless suppression of the uprising by the direct intervention of massive Soviet forces showed Moscow's determination to reassert its domination over Hungary, once events and popular feelings had swept over the heads of the "national" Communists. In any case, the recent course of Khrushchev and Co. suggests an extremely nonchalant attitude toward the possible repercussions of their own ideological pronouncements.

If the Soviet leadership is finally driven, no matter how reluctantly, to grant organizational and ideological auton-

omy to all Soviet satellites, the only remaining force binding them to Moscow will be a common core of shared
beliefs. Some observers argue that a federation of Communist states which had rid itself of the great bulk of Marxist-
Leninist dogma and had reduced its Communist orthodoxy
to a streamlined core of doctrine might turn out to be a
more formidable force than Stalin's tightly controlled empire. The question remains: What is this enduring hard
core of doctrine? Over the last thirty years much has fallen
by the wayside that was once considered essential doctrine.
Is there at present any core on which China, Yugoslavia,
and Gomulka's Poland will be able to agree? In the decisive
days of November 1956 Gomulka announced that not only
would Poland's path to socialism differ, but Polish socialism would be radically different from the Russian variety.

The risk, newly emphasized by the popular uprising in
Hungary, that "national Communism" represents an unstable compromise, may lead the leaders of Communist
China, Poland, and Yugoslavia to bethink themselves. It
may lead them to stress the need for preserving a normative
common core of doctrine, uniform for all Communist regimes. Whether such a core can be found is now open to
question. Whether, even if found, it can be maintained in
a world of autonomous Communist states is even more
questionable.

In spite of the gradual disintegration of shared Communist orthodoxy, the immediate prospects for the relations
between Moscow and Peking do not necessarily point to
any "break." Over recent years, Soviet policy has moved
steadily toward an increasing recognition, first, of China's
organizational and, then, of its ideological autonomy. The
potential pressure toward "Titoism" has thus been released
in time. Furthermore, in the present state of the world, the
Chinese Communist leaders are probably as anxious as the
Kremlin itself to preserve a common core of Communist

doctrine, in spite of their own manipulations of the ideology. At the same time, the drastic disintegration of the ideology—a disintegration to which the Chinese party has contributed substantially—has greatly weakened ideology as a binding fabric, not only between Moscow and Peking, but among all the states of the Communist world.

3

LET THE HUNDRED FLOWERS BLOOM
(1957)

In surveying the series of striking ideological pronouncements which have emanated from Communist China during the last year or so, there are certain questions which come to mind. What are the pressures which lie behind these pronouncements? What are some of the basic points which have been made and to what extent can they be said to contain basic novelties when viewed in the light of Soviet ideological developments? What, if any, has been the operational significance of these pronouncements? Have they merely been made in response to current pressures or do they reflect long-term historic tendencies of the Chinese Communist movement under its present leadership?

It is not difficult to discern some of the current pressures —both domestic and foreign—which lie behind them. The whole post-Stalin development in the Soviet Union—the events in Poland and Hungary—have obviously played

NOTE: This essay was first published under the title "Some Speculations on Ideological Shifts in Communist China" in *Problems of Communism,* July-August 1957.

their role. Mao's speech of February 27, 1957, even in its edited form, betrays a deep concern with Hungarian events. On the domestic side, the effort to apply a Stalinist model of economic development has clearly entered troubled waters. When the slogan "Let the hundred flowers bloom; let the hundred schools contend" was first proclaimed last year, it was explicitly stated that one of its purposes was to encourage the initiative of the nonparty intelligentsia. The appreciation of the professional talents of this class certainly rose sharply with the growing sense of crisis in many areas. On the other hand, it seems to me that the view expressed in some quarters that the recent ideological shifts are wholly a response to the acute economic crisis in China or that a state of revolt of Hungarian proportions was imminent should be viewed with skepticism. Can the present economic situation or sufferings of the masses be much worse than those of the Soviet Union during the early five-year-plan period? In spite of the infinite sufferings of that period the Soviet regime had developed potent instruments sufficient to prevent the crisis from having any political consequences. It would certainly appear that a government which has been able to gather such vast masses of peasants into producers cooperatives in so short a time has similar instruments available. It may be urged that events in other parts of the Communist world may have created in many strata of the Chinese population a far less compliant attitude toward the sufferings attendant upon a Stalinist model of industrial development. If this is so, it is a fact which reflects recent changes in climate in the Communist world as a whole and is not simply a result of the economic crisis per se. It is, however, possible that the leadership itself—particularly Mao—has become more and more uneasy about meeting economic difficulties in 1957 in precisely the same manner in which Stalin met them in the early thirties, even though the machinery for doing so is at hand.

On the whole, therefore, I would be inclined to surmise that to the extent that these ideological shifts are a response to current pressures, the pressures are those of the whole international situation—and particularly the situation in the Communist world—rather than those of purely domestic origin.[1] Furthermore, while these shifts may represent a response to current pressures, some of them may also represent the culmination of trends long latent in the Maoist version of Marxist-Leninist ideology. The current situation may, in some respects, merely have provided a more propitious climate for a bolder and more explicit statement of conclusions already implicit in previously held notions. I shall discuss this problem further below.

When we turn to the content of the shifts, we find that among the major pronouncements are those on the slogan "Let the hundred flowers bloom; let the hundred schools contend"[2] and Mao's speeches of February 27 and March 12 of this year. The June 1956 speech on the "Historic Significance of the Dictatorship of the Proletariat" and the December statement on "More on the Historic Significance of the Dictatorship of the Proletariat" do not, at first view, seem congruent with the spirit of these ideological shifts. Indeed, the statement of December might even seem to run counter to the general drift of ideological change. This is a problem which will be briefly considered below.

The slogan "Let a hundred schools contend" is, of course, most obviously directed to the intelligentsia. Its promulgation follows fairly closely upon a typical Stalinist type of ideological heresy-hunting campaign directed

[1] My own present inclination, in retrospect, is to give somewhat more weight to the domestic situation than here indicated.

[2] One of the first and most authoritative statements on this subject may be found in Lu Ting-yi's speech of May 26, 1956. For the text of the speech see *Communist China 1955–1959: Policy Documents with Analysis*, with a foreword by Robert R. Bowie and John K. Fairbank (Cambridge, Mass.: Harvard University Press, 1962), pp. 151–163.

against the literary figure Hu Feng and that favorite "bourgeois" target, Hu Shih. As indicated, it undoubtedly reflects a change in view on how to treat the intelligentsia given the current situation. On the other hand, a careful reading of Lu Ting-yi's speech of May 26, 1956, indicates that many of the assumptions which were to be made explicit in Mao's later speeches are already present in this pronouncement. It may thus be considered an organic part of the whole ideological shift which has since transpired.

On the basis of Lu's speech,[3] what can be said concerning the scope and limits of the free market of ideas which is here being proclaimed? As Lu points out, the phrase "hundred schools" is an allusion to the hundred schools of philosophy which flourished during the Chou dynasty before Confucianism was made the official philosophy. It was, indeed, a period of great and genuine freedom of thought. Lu hastens to add, however, that while the philosophic conflicts of the Chou period represented deep contradictions among contending social classes, in present-day China such a contention among the hundred schools will take place "under the conscious direction of the people." Here we note already the difference between nonantagonistic contradictions "within the people" and antagonistic contradictions of a society where genuine irreconcilable class struggle exists. We also note that "the people" is treated as an organic unit.

However, while "the people" is an organic unity, it is still made up of four social classes—proletariat, peasantry, petty bourgeoisie, and national bourgeoisie—so that there are also "elements of disunity" in the people. Each of these classes continues to exude its own characteristic ideology in spite of the great progress which has been made in the ideological transformation of all the classes. Because they be-

[3] The speech is probably a typical party interpretation close to Mao's. Other differing interpretations have also appeared.

long to the people, these classes are educable. Their ideological sickness (a favorite metaphor of Mao) is subject to therapy. The therapy should, however, not include terror or "crude coercive methods." If they have "idealistic" attitudes, these attitudes will not be cured by suppressing them. Furthermore, the expression of such views will prevent Marxism-Leninism from becoming a "hot-house plant." In some sense, by a dialectic process (Mao's mind is obsessed by the imagery of the dialectic as he understands it), these flowers, noxious and otherwise, may even help to enrich Marxism-Leninism.

It is, however, important to note at this point that it is not simply a question of the content of the ideas but of who advocates them. When an "idealistic" notion is advocated by a "member of the people" it is legitimate. The same idea advocated by an "enemy" or an "unmistakable counterrevolutionary" is inadmissible. The power of determining who is a member of the people and who is a counterrevolutionary lies firmly in the hands of the people's government. What is more, there is no guarantee that a particular idea may not prove, in the government's view, so noxious and so "revisionist" that it may remove its advocate from the category of the people to the category of the enemy. It is thus by no means clear that the government is indifferent to the content of ideas.

While one of the aims of the Hundred Flowers movement is to bring to the surface some of the false ideas which are normally present in the people, perhaps even more interesting is the implication that in the area of arts and sciences there should be something like a genuine free market of ideas. The novelty here is that Marxism-Leninism as interpreted by the party may not at any given point in time even have a clear-cut view on what is right or wrong in this area. Lu Ting-yi is quite radical on this subject. "The natural sciences," he states, "have no class nature." While Stalin himself proclaimed that there are spheres of culture—language in particular—which belong neither to the substructure nor to the superstructure, the natural sciences have never been assigned to this sphere. In the area of literature, Lu stipulates that while literature must "serve the workers, peasants, and soldiers," "socialist realism" may not be the only creative methodology which serves this purpose.

Mao's statement of February 27 also stresses the significance of the slogan for the realm of art and science. "Different forms and styles in art can develop freely and different schools in science can contend freely . . . Questions of right and wrong in the arts and sciences should be settled through free discussion in artistic and scientific circles." [4] While all this seems to recognize a certain autonomy for science and a somewhat lesser autonomy for art, one must again be on one's guard for all sorts of equivocations and loaded words. Again the decision whether any given form of art "serves the people" clearly belongs to the political leaders. Since party personnel occupy strategic places in artistic and scientific circles, one may well have one's doubts about the freedom of discussion even within these circles themselves. There is nothing to prevent the leaders from deciding that a given matter being agitated in the sphere of art or science actually is very relevant to vital areas of Marxism-Leninism. No institutionalized guarantees of freedom are granted.

Nevertheless, while Mao has not really relinquished the state's totalitarian powers within these areas, there may be a genuine desire to hold the state's totalitarian powers in reserve, as it were, within these areas. Whether the "holding in reserve" actually will mean a relinquishment of ultimate spiritual authority in the natural sciences, it is still too early to say.

[4] "On the Correct Handling of Contradictions among the People," *Communist China 1955–1959,* p. 288.

Leaving aside for a moment the question of the operational significance of these slogans, how do they relate themselves to Soviet ideology? Now there is one form in which "idealistic" error is "tolerated" in the U.S.S.R.—the form of religion. There has been no notion, however, that other forms of "bourgeois idealism" should be allowed free expression as a "normal" aspect of Soviet society. Soviet "socialist" society is presumably a classless society, and as such the Soviet "people" can have only one legitimate ideology—the correct Marxist-Leninist ideology. To the extent that erroneous ideas continue to persist, these ideas are not expressions of groups which form an organic part of the people but are either capitalist remnants in the minds of the people or the result of sinister influences from the enemy abroad. To the extent that there has been any "loosening" in the Soviet Union, it has presumably all taken place within the framework of Marxism-Leninism.[5] The only procedure against false ideology is to track it down and eliminate it. Religion alone, as a peculiarly stubborn remnant, must be dealt with by slower methods. There has also been no hint that Marxism-Leninism requires the constant stimulus of hostile ideas in order to retain its creativity. The Communist Party presumably possesses sufficient inner resources to provide whatever self-correction or self-criticism is necessary.

Now while the slogan "Let the hundred flowers bloom; let the hundred schools contend" actually appeared some time before Mao's pronouncements of February 27 and March 12, it presupposes many of the assumptions which are finally made explicit in Mao's speeches. Many of these assumptions, furthermore, have earlier historic roots.

What are some of these basic assumptions?

(1) That in China, "socialism" is being built by the "people" as a whole and the "people" is still defined as being

---

[5] Even if the most heinous heresies are proclaimed, they will be proclaimed in the name of Marxism-Leninism.

made up of four social classes—proletariat, peasantry, petty bourgeoisie, and "national" bourgeoisie. It is, of course, being built under the leadership of the Communist Party. Strictly speaking, the Communist Party itself is still the party of the industrial proletariat. It is not actually stated that the Communist Party embodies the general will of the whole people (although one occasionally sees statements which seem to imply this). Of course, as in the Soviet Union, the party is presumed to represent the interests of the "toiling peasantry" as well as of the proletariat. However, the whole apparatus of democratic parties and of such organs as the Chinese People's Political Consultative Conference—an apparatus which has figured very prominently in recent months—presumably represents those elements of the "people" not organically represented by the Communist Party. Mao Tse-tung himself is, of course, not only the head of the Communist Party, but also of the people's government as a whole. One might say that the whole tendency of his recent thought is to magnify the importance of the latter role at the expense of the former.

If we compare this to Soviet doctrine concerning the Soviet Union, we find that the Soviet social system is defined as that of a classless society. The Communist Party represents the interests of the proletariat, the working intelligentsia which is, as it were, an appendage of the working class and the working peasantry. It is interesting to note in this connection that in China, a large part of the nonparty intelligentsia is still assigned to the bourgeoisie. Hence, the presumption is that while the Soviet intelligentsia is by social definition wholly committed to Marxism-Leninism, a certain amount of ideological error is still considered "normal" as far as the Chinese intelligentsia is concerned. It is also interesting to note that recently a Chinese publication stated that even after classes have disappeared in China qua classes, the apparatus of united front government will still be necessary since the former classes will become different interest groups, and different interests may still require their own representation.

(2) The assumption that the whole "people" can build socialism rests on the assumption that all the classes of the people are subject to spiritual transformation by education and "persuasion." Their ideological sickness can be cured by proper therapy. The speech of February 27 carries this whole notion to its logical conclusion. "All classes, strata, and social groups that approve, support, and work for the cause of socialist construction belong to the category of the people." [6] The people then must ultimately be defined in terms of its conscious attitudes. This means that even though the "people" and "the enemy" are separate organisms, the membrane between them is highly porous. Presumably Chiang Kai-shek along with the Taiwan government could pass over from the class of the enemy to the people were he to develop proper attitudes toward "socialist transformation." "Revisionists," on the other hand, may pass from the ranks of the people to those of the enemy.

Part of the therapy, however, lies in the recognition that so long as "the people" includes classes like the petty bourgeoisie and national bourgeoisie, it will continue to exude idealist ideology. The best way to cure the ailment is to allow this ideology to express itself while carrying on a constant treatment in terms of ideological transformation.

(3) From this there follows the assumption that nonantagonistic contradictions are both normal and desirable among the people, even in a socialist society. Now the concept of antagonistic versus nonantagonistic contradictions is actually of Soviet origin. In the Soviet Union, it was probably first used in the realm of literature in order to introduce some sense of conflict, and it has been stated that

6 "On the Correct Handling of Contradictions," p. 276.

there are nonantagonistic contradictions between the forces of production and relations of production. What is novel in the Chinese case is not the concept but the use to which it has been put. The idea that the contradictions between the national bourgeoisie (an exploiting class) and the proletariat are nonantagonistic is a notion for which Soviet ideology does not provide. It is nevertheless a notion which is quite consistent with the other assumptions considered above.

(4) The assumption that there may be nonantagonistic contradictions between the "leaders" and the people. Here again, as in the case of contradictions within the people, the fleeting contradictions are presumed to rest on a bedrock of preestablished harmony.

What is new in this notion? The notion that "bureaucrats" (by which is generally meant the lower echelons) may be in conflict with the people is certainly not new in either the Soviet Union or China. The notion that contradictions may exist between the outlook of the "vanguard" and of the "masses" is not new and can already be found in Lenin. The vanguard, armed with Marxist-Leninist doctrine, surveys the historic scene from its heights and can see the larger, long-term picture. The masses are bound by their limited, partial views and their devotion to their own self-interest. What is new here is the fact that the vague word "leaders" is used rather than "bureaucrats." Presumably not only lower bureaucrats but the whole Communist Party and even Mao himself may be involved in contradiction with the masses. It has already been conceded that Stalin had fallen into subjectivist errors. In the contradiction between the "leaders" and the "people" there may be occasions on which the "leaders" are wrong. Their views may at times be too remote from the immediate interests of the people.

Since the possibility is here contemplated that the Communist Party as a whole may occasionally lapse from its in-fallibility, the party should be exposed to criticism from other parties and groups. While it is true that generally speaking the Communist Party is the custodian of Marxist-Leninist truth, while the other democratic groups are still infected with bourgeois error, on given concrete matters it is not inconceivable that their criticism is justified.

With regard to the position of Mao himself, the general possibility of his being wrong does arise. However, Mao is again not only the leader of the Communist Party but also the leader of the people. By identifying himself occasionally with the "people" rather than with the party, he can him-self, as it were, criticize the party from without.[7]

Now while all these assumptions may be said to represent further shifts away from previous orthodoxy, the fact re-mains that on one point of doctrine, the year 1956 actually saw what seems to be a reversal to Soviet orthodoxy.

During the whole period from Yenan until 1956, the Chinese Communists had stubbornly refused to state that China would require a "dictatorship of the proletariat" in its period of transition to socialism. In the June statement on the "Historic Experience of the Dictatorship of the Proletariat," however, we find it explicitly stated that the Chinese people's democratic dictatorship is a form of dic-tatorship of the proletariat.[8] Behind this lies a complex history of ideological relationships with the Soviet Union. The Soviet leaders—including Khrushchev—have insisted on the retention of the phrase "dictatorship of the prole-tariat" as constituting the indispensable heart of Leninism. In effect, what they indicated to the Chinese at the time of the Twentieth Congress was that the Chinese were entirely

[7] It is interesting to note that in this respect the "Hundred Flowers" campaign anticipates the "Great Proletarian Cultural Revolution."

[8] For a further discussion of this issue, see No. 2, "Communist Ide-ology and the Sino-Soviet Alliance."

109

free to construe this phrase in any way they saw fit, provided that they kept the phrase. Here we have one of those cases in which a phrase itself is important even if emptied of all substance. By June of 1956 the Chinese proved willing to accept this compromise. The events in Hungary may in fact have convinced them that this was a wise decision. They too, like the Soviets, are interested in preserving an inviolable core of shared doctrine or at least shared phraseology. Yet the adoption of this phrase has had little effect on the course of ideological development. It is in fact quite interesting to note that the published version of Mao's February speech does not include one reference to the dictatorship of the proletariat.[9]

Operational Significance. What, if any, have been the operational consequences of these shifts within China?

In a speech delivered before the People's Political Consultative Conference, March 18, 1957, the "democratic personage" Lo Lung-ch'i complains that "during the last year not many flowers bloomed and few schools of thought contended in the academic and ideological fields . . . the basic cause here is that the higher intellectuals are still suspicious and are still plagued by misgiving." And well they might be. They have no assurance that they may not be reclassified at any moment from the status of member of the people to the status of enemy. They can never be sure whether any idea propounded by them is an expression of the normal bourgeois idealism of the people or when it may turn into "dangerous revisionism." Furthermore, there is the presumption that the intellectuals are making steady progress in their march away from "idealism" to a proper

[9] As indicated in the introductory essay, the phrase "dictatorship of the proletariat" is at present by no means entirely "empty of substance."

grasp of Marxism-Leninism. All this does not provide a very fertile soil for large varieties of floral vegetation.

What then, if any, are some of the possible operational consequences of this slogan? It is implied more strongly than in the past that physical coercion will not generally be used in ideological matters. When errors are found in assertions which are purportedly orthodox, they will be treated less severely. It is strongly implied that in the natural sciences a wider play will be allowed. In literature one may try new approaches—at some risk. Within the official ideology more play will be allowed on certain predesignated academic questions. One may know somewhat more about "bourgeois thought" (for example, that of Keynes in economics). It is possible that Mao has more in mind than this. If so, this has not yet become manifest in current Chinese literature.

If we turn to the whole area of contradictions within the people and contradictions between the people and the leaders, it is also difficult to discern as yet any sweeping consequences. The so-called democratic parties and the People's Political Consultative Conference have, it is true, probably greatly risen in prestige. They have been given tremendous publicity and have been the object of particular attention. Conversely, the very notion that there should be "mutual supervision" between the democratic parties and the Communist Party inevitably lowers that party somewhat from its dazzling heights. This is true even if we assume that the democratic parties are as firmly controlled from on top as the Communist Party itself. We know that there has in fact been criticism of the Communist Party by people in the democratic parties. We also know that this criticism has already been called "excessive." So far, the main effect of the notion of contradiction between "leaders" and "people" has been a conventional attack on bureaucratism couched in the language of thought remolding.

These ideological drifts may yet have spectacular consequences in China's domestic development (perhaps even consequences unforeseen by the leadership). If Mao and those in his entourage wish to restrict their operational consequence to as narrow an area as possible, the slippery language of these pronouncements makes it possible to do so.

In terms of relationships with Moscow and the other parts of the Communist world, as well as in terms of relationships to uncommitted Asia, however, these shifts may have an enormous significance. More clearly than ever Mao proclaims his position as a theorist in his own right and, by the same token, emphasizes the unassailable ideological autonomy of Communist China. It is further implied that not only has the Chinese path to socialism differed from Moscow's, but that "socialism" itself may differ in China. In China socialism will be compatible with a multi-party government, and Chinese socialism will be more ready to recognize that even under socialism, there may arise real differences of interest among the various strata of the people. It is perhaps these implications which have particularly excited the Poles. To the peoples of Asia with their pitifully small proletariats, it announces that in China—as one Asian country—the whole "people" has built socialism without bitter and inexorable conflicts among the classes which compose the people. To Asian intellectuals, consumed by a resentful nationalism and favorably disposed to "socialism," this notion of a "populist" road to socialism may presumably make the Chinese path more attractive than the Soviet. The attack on "crude coercive methods" and the motto about the hundred schools—whatever its real meaning in China—implies that a totalitarian China can inoculate itself as it were with some of the advantages of political democracy (and there is a covert admission that there are such advantages) without abandoning its fundamental totalitarian control. Such a formula, whether viable or not, is perhaps quite attractive to a man like Gomulka.

This does not mean that Mao is not sincere in desiring the solidarity of the Communist world or not fundamentally hostile to the West. He will have such a solidarity, however, on his own terms—terms which involve a thoroughgoing organizational and ideological autonomy. If there is to be a common core of doctrine which all Communist states must share, he must have as much discretion in defining this core as anyone in the Kremlin. The notion that Mao wants to assume the leadership of the whole Communist world is perhaps not justified. At the same time, if the emerging Chinese conception of "socialism" should prove more attractive in some parts of the Communist world than Moscow's, this is not necessarily an unattractive prospect.

Historical Background and Ultimate Significance. Do any of the ideological shifts here considered have a past, or are they all responses to immediate pressures? Actually, there is a considerable history behind some of the notions which manifest themselves in Mao's statements. A drift toward the notion that "socialism" in China would be built by the whole "people"—that is, a drift away from a strictly class interpretation of the march of history to a sort of "populist" interpretation—begins at a very early date. It is, of course, true that the "people" is still defined as an assemblage of "classes," each with its own class interests and ideology. It is, in fact, the combination of the notion of a sort of "general will" of the people with the notion of class interests "within the people" which made possible Mao's recent pronouncement on nonantagonistic contradictions within the people.

The united front line of the Yenan period was, of course,

113

not in itself a manifestation of such a drift. The notion of a united front during the "bourgeois democratic" period is, of course, by no means new in Communist ideology. However, even in Yenan days and in the immediate post-war period, Mao occasionally hinted that in China the whole "people," including the national bourgeoisie, would be "educated" to an acceptance of socialism. Mao's speech on the "People's Democratic Dictatorship" in 1949 hints it even more strongly, as does the constitution of 1954.

Viewing the drift from the point of view of the history of Communist ideology in general, one may say that a tension between a strictly Marxist class interpretation and a sort of "populist" interpretation can already be found in Lenin himself. Nor has Mao by any means abandoned all the clichés of class analysis. What we note here, however, is an underlying tendency which has become considerably accelerated within the Chinese context.

Closely allied to the tendency toward a "populist" interpretation of Chinese totalitarianism is the tremendous insistence on the potentialities of "ideological remolding" and "thought reform." The whole "people" can build "socialism" precisely because the whole people can be spiritually transformed by proper educational (and therapeutic) methods. The whole emphasis on "ideological remolding" and "thought reform" through "persuasion," which ultimately led to all the refinements of "brainwashing," had its beginnings in the Yenan days. At first, to be sure, the methods were applied in a much narrower sphere. It was more a question of turning the intellectuals, semi-intellectuals, and peasants who made up the Communist Party into "spiritual" proletarians, as it were. It was after 1949 that the methods used in "molding" good Communists out of presumably recalcitrant material were applied to the "people" as a whole. Long before February 27, the doctrine was proclaimed that *ultimately*, whole classes such as the peasantry, petty bourgeoisie, and national bourgeoisie could be reeducated and cured. They could only be cured, however, if their deep-layed ideological ailments were brought to the surface. To some extent, the whole "let the hundred schools contend" drive fits into the framework of this therapeutic process, although it is also presumed to have more positive aspects.

Here again one cannot view the whole Chinese experience in isolation from previous Soviet developments. With Lenin himself consciousness comes to play a role never contemplated by Marx. Nevertheless, the notion of the transformation of whole social classes (including the "bourgeoisie") by educative methods marks another step forward in the disintegration of the doctrine. It is this assumption, above all, which made possible Mao's recent pronouncements.

What, then, is the overall vision offered in Mao's speeches? It is the vision of a totalitarian society by consent, as it were, and of a totalitarian society in which the state may hold its authority in reserve in certain well-defined areas of culture (such as natural science). The "fundamental" harmony of the society will be preserved all the more effectively by allowing an area of slack—by recognizing that certain clashes of interest are normal, that a certain degree of ideological error is normal, and that there may be certain areas of the arts and sciences where Marxism-Leninism does not immediately yield any answers, even though the authority of the state remains supreme.

The concept remains fundamentally totalitarian. The leaders still embody the fundamental interests of the people apart from any institutions of political democracy. No institutional check on the power of the leaders is contemplated in any area. The leaders determine who belongs to the category of the "people" and who has gone over to the "enemy." The leaders determine what types of flowers shall bloom and what types of vegetation are so poisonously revisionist that they must be uprooted. In the contradiction between "leaders" and "people," it is clear where the ultimate discretion lies, although it is not impossible that at times Mao may align himself with the "people" against the "party."

The areas in which "contradictions" are possible remain hazy. The definition of "normal" error remains hazy. All formulae remain so vague that the government can use them to encourage a real and wide-ranging freedom in the marketplace of ideas or can use them to retreat to the situation as it existed before 1956. It may also use them to create—as it seems to be doing at present—certain contrived, intentional deviations.

Quite apart from the domestic use of these formulae, however, they remain significant for what they are intended to suggest to the countries of the Communist world and the countries of noncommitted Asia. Above all they confirm more decisively than ever the total ideological autonomy of Communist China.

4

CHINA AND THE COMMUNIST BLOC:
A SPECULATIVE RECONSTRUCTION (1958)

The history of the Chinese Communist state since its assumption of power in 1949 has hardly been marked by the smooth continuities which so delight the heart of the professional historian. Sudden lurches and sharp turns from one "mass campaign" to another have been the constant earmark of these scant nine years of the regime's history. If one stands back one can perhaps discern certain master trends below the surface—such as the overriding tendency toward the establishment of ever greater totalitarian control. Yet even a discernment of master trends will not help one to anticipate the next sharp turn on the domestic and international front.

Since the beginning of 1956 these lurches and turns seem to have gained momentum. The anti-Hu-Feng campaign was followed by the "Let the Hundred Flowers Bloom" campaign. This was followed by the frenzied anti-rightist campaign which has blended with the "leap forward" in

NOTE: This essay was first published in *Current History*, vol. 35, no. 208 (December 1958).

productions goals, the emphasis on small local enterprises, and finally the almost mystical ultra-collectivism of the "people's communes" with its intimations that "Communist" society is at hand. The anti-rightist campaign was rounded off this year by the anti-Tito campaign and at the present time the dominant theme is the reactivation of the Quemoy-Matsu issue.

Where do the roots of these unending shifts lie? Are the factors which lie behind these shifts mainly domestic or do considerations of intra-bloc relations and international relations in general play some role? Are they all the outward manifestations of some unfolding master plan or have unforeseen contingencies and surprise played some role? If one assumes that the erratic development arises wholly out of domestic considerations, the notion of the unfolding master plan becomes more plausible. One may assume that the top leadership has by now achieved an impressive control of domestic affairs even though unforeseen contingencies and pressures undoubtedly may still arise.

However, if one assumes that many of these shifts must be related to events in other parts of the Communist orbit or in the world in general, the notion of the unfolding master plan becomes highly doubtful. With all due respect to Mao Tse-tung's sagacity, there is no evidence that he anticipated the events in Poland or Hungary or Tito's attitude to the Moscow Conference of 1957 or many other events on the international scene.

Actually, within a Communist context, it would be highly artificial to draw a sharp line of demarcation between the three areas of domestic development, bloc relations, and international relations. To the extent that the Chinese Communist regime operates within the framework of assumptions common to the orbit as a whole, anything which happens to ideology or the sociopolitical system of communism elsewhere within the bloc must affect ideological control at home. There is every evidence that, in the past two years in particular, the Chinese Communist regime has become acutely aware of the possible impact of events in the bloc as a whole on domestic affairs of China.

On the other hand, the Stalinist model of forced industrialization in China itself can hardly be divorced from the fanatical will to achieve great power status whatever may be its other presumed goals. Thus, while we may concede domestic factors a certain priority, they are hopelessly enmeshed with factors of intra-bloc and international politics. The unfolding master plan may exist but it is constantly vulnerable to disruption by the unforeseen contingencies of events outside of China.

In the following pages a tentative attempt will be made to reconstruct speculatively some of the considerations which may have lain behind the zigzag course of China's policies during the last two years, particularly as such policies affect intra-bloc relationships.

The Twentieth Congress of the CPSU undoubtedly marked an important point in Sino-Soviet relations. It marked the triumph of Khrushchev's policy of deference to China's assertion of its own organizational and ideological autonomy. The peculiarities of the Chinese path to socialism were endorsed. In return for this endorsement, however, Moscow was able to obtain an ideological counterconcession.[1] After having avoided for many years the application of the term "dictatorship of the proletariat" to the Chinese development, the Chinese now conceded that the Chinese "path to socialism" was a subvariety of the "dictatorship of the proletariat." There seems to have been a mutual agreement that this verbal formula must remain a vital element of the Communist ideological baggage.

While the Twentieth Congress undoubtedly reinforced

[1] For a fuller discussion of this, see No. 2, "Communist Ideology and the Sino-Soviet Alliance."

Sino-Soviet ties, there seems little reason to assume that Moscow had as yet promoted Peking to a position of partnership in intra-bloc affairs. Furthermore, even after the Twentieth Congress, Peking continued to stress the danger of "great power chauvinism" quite as much as the opposite danger of disintegration due to the corrosion of the remaining core of accepted dogma. There was still a disposition to welcome the assertion of greater autonomy on the part of the European satellites, thus linking Peking's interests within the bloc to the interest of these non-Soviet states.

All the available evidence would indicate that in the early phase of the Polish events Peking looked with a cautiously benign eye on Poland's assertion of a degree of independence. This evidence can be found not only in the reports of such Polish visitors as Ochab and Cyrankiewicz, but also in the official Chinese Communist press itself. This guarded approval may not have been directed to the substantive changes brought about by the Polish events in Poland so much as to the mere fact of the assertion of independence. Even the first stage of the Hungarian revolution does not seem to have aroused Peking's active hostility. On the contrary the striking role of the intelligentsia (in the larger Communist sense of the word) in both the Polish and Hungarian events seems to have led to second thoughts about the position of China's own much-harried intelligentsia. It is conceivable that it was the Polish events and the earliest phase of the Hungarian developments more than anything else which lay behind the whole "Hundred Flowers" episode in China itself.

"The Hundred Flowers." As the "Hundred Flowers" episode recedes in time, the question of its proper interpretation becomes increasingly difficult. Was the whole campaign inspired by purely domestic considerations or did it represent a response to events in the Communist bloc? Above

all, was it really designed to give the intelligentsia some sense of added freedom, however narrowly defined, or was it purely an effort to "smoke out" the opposition? The latter interpretation is seemingly supported by the whole subsequent anti-rightist development.

During the period preceding "the hundred flowers" episode, the Chinese intelligentsia had been subject to the extreme rigors of the anti-Hu-Feng campaign and there were many indications that it was not in a particularly spirited mood at the beginning of 1956. It is thus likely that the problem of rousing the energies of the intelligentsia in China, coinciding with the revelations of the Polish and Hungarian events, may well have led Mao and others to the view that some sort of release of the safety valve was called for in this situation. Mao's speech of February 1957, even in its edited and revised form, reveals a deep concern with events in Hungary.[2]

A close study of the documents bearing on the "Hundred Flowers" campaign reveals that the areas of freedom were never well defined. The formulae in terms of which a certain area for maneuver was granted were extremely vague and left open the door at any moment to a reversal of policy. It would appear that neither Mao nor those in his entourage expected any major heterodoxy to appear in those areas which affected vital state policies. The intelligentsia had after all undergone an arduous course of thought reform and should have known the proper line separating "antagonistic" from "nonantagonistic" contradictions.

The assumption we are making, therefore, is that the hundred flowers campaign was not exclusively a "smoking out" operation although one may assume that the leadership was extremely interested in discovering what types of

[2] For the text of this speech, see *Current History*, December 1957.

flowers would sprout. It is interesting to note that the Chinese Communists themselves have on the one hand tended to support the "smoking out" interpretation and on the other to maintain that the hundred flowers are still blooming even today.

It is however precisely this Communist adherence to the "smoking out" theory which makes it suspicious. If one assumes that the hundred flowers campaign was an exploratory effort in the direction of granting the intelligentsia a certain undefined limited area of maneuverability, this leads to an image of Mao Tse-tung as a man capable of being troubled, bewildered, and surprised. The "smoking out" theory is much more in keeping with the hagiographic image of a Mao always self-possessed and never surprised.

It was, of course, in the very midst of the hundred flowers campaign that the Hungarian Communist regime showed signs of advanced decay. It was now revealed that the drive for more autonomy might in certain instances lead to the very collapse of a Communist regime. It is by no means clear however, that the Hungarian events in and of themselves led to the decision to reverse the whole hundred flowers enterprise. The Chinese leadership was clearly deeply troubled by these events but still seemed to equivocate during the early months of 1957 concerning the lessons to be drawn from them. The treachery of Nagy might be condemned but might not the emergence of treacherous revisionism have been a direct result of Rakosi "doctrinarism"?

The Chinese politbureau statement of December 29, 1956, is still enormously equivocal and troubled although it leans in the direction of stressing the dangers of revisionism. The revised version of Mao's speech "On Contradictions" of February 1957 is on one hand, an exposition of the hundred flowers doctrine and, on the other, a careful explanation of the limits of this doctrine. The unequivocal decision to drop the whole hundred flowers enterprise and mercilessly suppress all manifestations of heterodoxy among the intelligentsia was probably due to the extraordinary behavior of certain elements among the Chinese intelligentsia itself and even among the students who continued to make political demands of the most shocking nature. It is possible that by the spring of 1957 the campaign had actually been converted into a "smoking out" operation.

Chinese-Russian Relations. Meanwhile, the same Polish and Hungarian events which may have led to the hundred flowers campaign within China were also leading to a striking transformation in relations between Peking and Moscow. The troubles of 1956 led both Moscow and the satellites to look to Peking as an arbiter of their differences. Peking was thrust into the center of the stage by the very force of circumstances. Poland and Hungary eagerly looked to Peking for support of their separate "paths to socialism." Khrushchev, who had shown such deference for the Chinese point of view, undoubtedly felt that he had reason to look for support in this direction in the midst of his mounting troubles. At the end of 1956, we saw Chou En-lai's active intervention in Polish and Hungarian affairs. By the end of 1957, Peking was promoted to a position of partnership in adjudicating the affairs of the bloc as a whole. This position of coleadership within the bloc, while reducing still further Peking's lingering fear of "great power chauvinism," radically changed its position vis-à-vis the other members of the Soviet bloc. The dangers to the solidarity of the bloc now became as much the responsibility of Peking as of Moscow.

In brief, then, the collapse of Hungarian Communism, the shocking demonstration of the unreliability of elements of the intelligentsia at home, and China's rise to a position of partnership within the Communist bloc probably suffice to explain Peking's turn to the hard line both at home and within the Communist bloc. If we add to this the demonstration of Soviet technological advance evinced by Sputnik and the recession in the United States, we may surmise that Mao Tse-tung set off for Moscow in November 1957 not only firmly convinced that the line must be held, but also in the firm conviction that, as he put it, "The East Wind was beginning to prevail over the West Wind."

If the impression of Sputnik was able to efface the impression of Hungary from the Western mind, this must be true a fortiori for a man with Mao's image of the world. Whatever flexibility Mao has shown in the course of dealing with complexities within China, his image of the outside world is probably still heavily conditioned by the stereotypes of doctrine.

One of the main tasks of the Moscow Conference of November 1957 was undoubtedly to formulate a common core of orthodoxy that would henceforth be mandatory for all Communist countries. There is every reason to believe that Mao himself played an active role in defining this core. It includes features such as the indispensability of the leading role of Communist parties in the achievement of socialism, the necessity of collectivization, and so forth.

In the light of this development, the violent reaction of Peking during the past year to Tito's stubborn recalcitrance becomes quite comprehensible. At a time when the emphasis must be on bloc solidarity; at a time when the declaration of a minimal core of shared orthodoxy is most urgent; at a time when, in Mao's view, the Communist bloc was beginning to show new strength vis-à-vis the non-Communist world, Tito refused to accept the irreducible core of orthodoxy and continued to propound notions that Peking had never accepted but which were now more impertinent and annoying than ever. Peking had never accepted the Titoist notion that in some societies socialism may be achieved under auspices other than those of the Communist Party or the Titoist experiment with "workers committees." One of the central planks of the Moscow declaration of 1957 was precisely the assertion that "the leadership of the Communist Party" in the transition to socialism is one of the universal fundamentals of Communist doctrine. Tito's defiance is no longer the defiance of Moscow alone. It is the defiance of the Moscow-Peking partnership. Having defined the essential elements of Communism, at least for the moment, Peking is convinced that those who do not accept this minimal definition should not be privileged to bear the name of Communist.

Yet the story does not end at this point. In spite of Peking's insistence on the imposition of a minimum core of orthodoxy on the Communist bloc, it has not renounced its own prerogative of carrying on further experiments along the "path to socialism" and now, it would appear, even along "the path to Communism." As a partner of Moscow, Peking has arrogated to itself a privilege which Moscow has long enjoyed—namely the right to impose dogma on others while allowing itself to carry on whatever experiments it deems necessary in its own interests.

In 1958 there have been striking experiments in China which, in some ways, carry China outside of the Stalinist model of socio-industrial development. These are by no means experiments in "liberalization." On the contrary, one might call them experiments in ultra-totalitarianism. While the pressures which lie behind these developments may not be ideological in the first instance, every effort has been made to place them within an ideological framework and to derive a maximum of ideological significance from them.

A New Confidence. Underlying these developments one notes the sudden access of an almost frenzied haste to

125

achieve the regime's goals as well as the appearance, at least, of an almost mystical self-confidence. The preconditions for this "leap forward" in the Chinese Communist account were created by the decisive defeat of "rightism" in the recent anti-rightist campaign. Having administered a decisive defeat to all sources of opposition, the regime is now able to consolidate and tap all the energies of China's vast population in a manner unanticipated hitherto.

In an oblique way, this may express a partial truth. Whatever sources of opposition may have existed among the academic or professional intelligentsia have certainly been crushed. The danger that this intelligentsia might be able to play a role approximating in any way the role of the Hungarian or Polish intelligentsia has been averted most effectively. On the other hand, there is little evidence that the masses in general played any role in the "Hundred Flowers" period. They seem to be under the firm control of the regime and, in the present mood of the leadership, may seem to be an infinitely malleable instrument in its hands. It is conceivable, however, that China's rise to a position of partnership within the Communist bloc has contributed to the present euphoria.

The two main innovations which have emerged are what Po I-po has called "China's new way of building industry" and the so-called "people's communes"—the latter a most recent development. The former involves the creation of vast numbers of small—even tiny—industrial enterprises in the countryside—enterprises designed to tap the limitless reservoir of peasant manpower. In every branch of production where operation on a small scale is possible (even including steel production) such enterprises are being created. The "leap forward" in the volume of industrial production which the leadership now claims to have achieved has presumably occurred largely in this sector. Whatever the economic implications of this development, it is being presented to the Communist bloc and to the world as a whole as yet another creative innovation of Chinese Communism to the storehouse of Marxist-Leninist experience.

In the ideological sphere it is maintained that since the Chinese peasants who "are not ordinary peasants" are now actually participating in industrial production, the lines between proletariat and peasantry are no longer sharply drawn. The transcendence of the distinction between worker and peasant, which is one of the prerequisites of the Communist stage of society, is actually being achieved in China.

The "people's communes," on the other hand, represent a consolidation of several cooperatives into one unit which will be both an economic and political unit. The commune will absorb the township government. On the other hand, ultra-collectivism will also be pushed downward. There will be "community dining rooms, kindergartens, nurseries, tailoring groups, barber shops, public baths, 'happy homes' for the aged, agricultural middle schools, 'red and expert' schools, etc." [3] The people, we read, "have taken to organizing themselves along military lines."

There again, the *primary* motives are probably economic and political. The consolidation of the cooperatives, the deepening and broadening of collectivist consolidation, may give the state a degree of control such as no totalitarian regime has ever known. However, the ideological framework which has been created for this development has a significance of its own. The "people's commune," we are informed, "will develop into the basic social unit in Communist society"—and "the attainment of communism in China is no longer a remote event." Presumably, the absorption of township government into the commune represents the withering away of the state on the level of local

[3] "Resolution on the Establishment of People's Communes in the Rural Areas," *Peking Review*, Sept. 16, 1958.

127

government and when this process has been completed "the function of the state will be limited to protecting the country from external aggression but will play no role internally."

It is possible that the whole mystique surrounding the "communes" may be reversed as a result of new circumstances. However, what Peking actually seems to be doing at the present time is devising a formula on the basis of which it may be able to promulgate the birth of Communism in China, at some time in the future. China, it would appear, is not only pursuing its own path to socialism, but also its own path to Communism. There are many interesting questions which might be raised concerning the relation of these innovations to the core of orthodox dogma which Peking has together with Moscow imposed on the Communist bloc. They may be considered by some as an exaggeration of orthodoxy. Yet they might also be considered highly heterodox. The important point to note here is that Peking has not allowed its position of responsibility within the Communist bloc to diminish its prerogative of manipulating ideology to suit its own purposes and of enhancing the impression of the peculiarly Chinese physiognomy of Chinese Communism.

If the past year may be considered a year of growing assertiveness on the part of Peking in every sphere, the reactivation of the Quemoy-Matsu problem must also be viewed in this context. Although China has achieved a partnership role in the Communist bloc, it is still held back from acting independently on the world scene by the constraints imposed by American policies. One need not suppose that if China could confront its main protagonist —the United States—on a direct basis rather than through the mediation of Moscow, its policies would necessarily diverge from those of the Soviet Union. It would however mean that Peking would confront the West on the same basis of full partnership on which it now confronts the Communist bloc. While Peking is undoubtedly genuinely interested in the recovery of Quemoy and Matsu, it is nevertheless conceivable that the larger aim which lies behind the whole agitation is the achievement of a more direct and independent confrontation with the West in general and the United States in particular.

5

SINO-SOVIET RELATIONS: THE QUESTION OF AUTHORITY (1963)

On the face of it, there seems little cause for wonder that two contiguous super nation-states should develop conflicts of interest. Those worldly philosophers who have always explained Sino-Soviet relations in terms of "hard" factors of national interest are finding little difficulty in enumerating the obvious divergencies of national interest which account for the current rift. It is, of course, true that many of the same worldly philosophers found little difficulty in the past in enumerating the "hard" factors which bound the Soviet Union and Communist China together in seemingly monolithic unity—for example, the common interest in ousting the United States from East Asia; the long common frontier, which has now become a point of conflict; the economic dependence of China on the Soviet Union; and so on.

Now it would, of course, be nonsense to deny that the Soviet Union and Communist China are nation-states in

NOTE: This essay was first published in *The Annals of the American Academy of Political and Social Science,* September 1963.

the broadest sense, each with a strong sense of self-identity, or that they are states which think in terms of national interest. One can hardly deny the presence of nationalism in both states. The nationalism of the Communist Chinese leadership is indeed virulent in intensity and its beginning can already be clearly discerned in the Yenan period. I would submit that the Mao Tse-tung of the early 1940's no longer views Chinese nationalism "from the outside" simply as a Leninist manipulator but from the inside as a Chinese nationalist. Indeed, viewed in secular terms, the general evolution of Communism may perhaps be described in terms of the gradual victory of the nation-state over Marxism-Leninism. The time may indeed come when the relations between the Soviet Union and Communist China may be adequately described wholly in terms of a national-interest calculus. I would simply urge that the time is not yet and that one should not describe the present in terms of plausible extrapolations of the future. It is not true as of the present that the syndrome of elements which we call Communism is *nothing but* the myth of Soviet nationalism or the myth of Chinese nationalism. To the extent that the two states have been bound together, the intensity of their bond had something to do with Communism. To the extent that they are drifting apart, the nature of the tension between them can not be understood apart from Communism. As a matter of fact, there is ample reason to believe that, at least on the Chinese side, the interest in Communist solidarity has, in the past, been sufficiently powerful to inhibit the assertion of national interests. The nationalist "irredentism" of the Chinese Communists has, in general, been maximalist in nature, yet the regime has, till now, sedulously refrained from reasserting the Chinese claim to Outer Mongolia. In the years immediately after 1949, it accepted without murmur, if not without chagrin, the Soviet special privileges in Manchuria, the Soviet rape of Manchurian industry, and the joint commercial enterprises. Recently, as we know, it has finally been openly hinted that China is no more reconciled to its present "imperialistically" imposed borders with the Soviet Union than it is to the Macmahon line. As the tension between the Soviet Union and Communist China becomes more exacerbated, the inhibitions on the assertion of the regime's conception of its nationalist interest become constantly more enfeebled. All the latent sources of conflict of national interest have, however, been present from the outset. I would, therefore, doubt whether they alone suffice to explain the contents of the pronunciamentos and fulminations which have been passing back and forth between Peking and Moscow.

If the calculators of national interests find nothing unusual in recent Sino-Soviet relations, there are, on the other hand, those who will settle for nothing less than the "profoundest" explanations of the current Sino-Soviet rift. There is already available a cluster of theories—anthropological, sociological, historical, and economic (economic-development theory)—designed to account particularly for the most recent developments in Sino-Soviet relations.

There are some who feel that the current relations between the Soviet Union and China can be understood only in terms of deep cultural differences which have their roots in the distant past. Now, while wholeheartedly accepting the view that Chinese and Russian cultures are profoundly different from each other—although there are, as we know, sociocultural theories, such as the theory of oriental despotism, which stress their fundamental similarity—and while granting that these differences may have a decisive effect on the future development of both societies, I see no need to invoke these differences in order to explain all aspects of Sino-Soviet relations during the last few years. There is much in the relations of political bodies which may be explained in terms of situational and general human factors—which would, in this case, include the conscious ideas of the protagonists—even where such political bodies are associated with different cultures. The effort to explain China's present international policies and posture in terms of Chinese culture may lead to a stress on precisely those strains in the culture which presumably favored the curent development. If there were counter tendencies within this millennial culture, these are not likely to be mentioned. The net result may be not an illumination of the present but a simplification of China's complex and turbulent past.

The problem of the past may itself be divided into two parts, at least as far as the Chinese are concerned. There is the past of the last century, which is by no means coterminous with "Chinese tradition." There can be no doubt whatever that the Chinese Communist movement has been profoundly shaped by the conditions which emerged in China during this period. The extreme nationalism of the Chinese Communists undoubtedly reflects the humiliations of the Chinese state during this period. The strategy developed by Mao Tse-tung cannot be understood apart from the phenomenon of regional militarism which dominates the whole period since 1911. There are many features of the historic situation in China before 1949 which facilitated the creation by the Chinese Communists of their own genuinely independent organization. This is, of course, a fact most immediately relevant to Sino-Soviet relations. Finally, there are many other features of the Chinese scene during the twentieth century which sharply differentiate China from Russia and which have continued to condition the responses of the Chinese leadership. Chinese industrial development was far behind that of Russia in 1917. China is an agrarian society in a much more overwhelming sense than was Russia, and China has had to confront a population problem of fearsome proportions. While all these are aspects of the situation differentiating China from Russia, they are by no means peculiar to "Chinese culture" and are general conditions shared with many "nondeveloped" agrarian societies.

When we turn to that past which can be described without reservation in terms of Chinese culture or Chinese tradition, it is probably quite true that this millennial culture will continue to shape the internal development of China and that many of its aspects may, in the long run, prove more durable than many aspects of Marxism-Leninism. It still profoundly influences the habits of thought and behavior of the Chinese Communist leadership, Mao Tse-tung in particular. The fact that China was, in the past, the center of a unique civilization may lend a certain intensity to its present nationalism not readily found elsewhere. The universalism of Confucianism may have created a disposition favorable to the universalistic claims of Marxism-Leninism. Yet, in the immediate scene, the fact that the positive content of Marxism-Leninism is in many ways entirely different from the positive content of Confucianism may be even more important than their common universalism. In dealing concretely with Sino-Soviet relations, I would urge that there is much that can still be explained in terms of the logic of power relations and with reference to the specificities of the uses of Marxist-Leninist ideology without invoking the whole of Chinese and Russian culture, even though these may be assumed to be pervasively present in both cases.

Another quite different type of "deep" explanation very much favored in the United States is that which explains Sino-Soviet differences in terms of stages of economic development. It is interesting that the Soviet writers have themselves begun to play with this theory. In the letter of the Communist Party of the Soviet Union to the Chinese

Communist Party published in *Pravda* on April 3, 1963, it is stated that "differing attitudes may arise on issues relating to domestic development and the international Communist movement and on forms and methods of our cooperation. This is possible, for the countries in the world socialist system find themselves at different stages in the building of the new society." Peking is, however, not likely to accept this explanation of its own position. It can, after all, point out that the Soviet Union has in its own development emphasized the "advantages of backwardness" and the notion that the last shall be first. In the West, the notion that Chinese "toughness" is a function of the fact that it is now in the "Stalinist stage of its industrialization process" while Soviet "moderation" is a result of its higher development wins ready assent among that vast host committed to what might be called the ideology of industrialism. Whether the whole conflict between the Soviet Union and China can be understood entirely in terms of the present issue of "hardness" and "moderation" is a question I should like to consider below. Whether, in fact, we really know anything about the supposed "functional" relation between stages of economic development and hardness or moderation of policy is an even more serious question. Soviet policy during the height of Stalinist development in the Soviet Union was isolationist and cautious. While Chinese policy has been consistent vis-à-vis the United States—as has been American policy vis-à-vis Communist China—its policy on other fronts has fluctuated within the limits set by Communism. There is no reason to believe that Communist China was in a less "Stalinist" phase of its development when it proclaimed the Bandung doctrine in its relations to the nonaligned world than it is now when it is committed to quite another approach. The economic power of the Soviet Union and the economic weakness of China undoubtedly condition the responses of the two leaderships in some fashion but do not necessarily dictate the particular policies adopted.

The Myth of the Communist Party. Many of the factors mentioned as well as those unmentioned undoubtedly enter in some way into the enormously complex skein of Sino-Soviet relations. I would nevertheless urge that one can still not understand these relations without reference to the realm known as Marxism-Leninism. It is not a question of seeking the center of gravity in "ideology" as such, for much of the sum total of ideology is by now dead letter and verbal ballast. There is, however, one point at which ideology still becomes directly related to power—becomes in itself a factor of power—that is, in the myth of the Communist Party. By the myth of the Communist Party, I refer not to the bare doctrine of organization but to the assumptions in terms of which the authority of the organization is legitimized. It is this myth, it seems to me, which remains at present the living heart of Marxism-Leninism. Whether the myth is genuinely believed or whether those whose power is based on it simply believe that its preservation is vital to the survival of their authority makes little difference in terms of practical consequence. The fact remains that the leaders of the Communist Party of the Soviet Union and of the Chinese Communist Party are not simply interested in those aspects of power involved with "national interests." They are perhaps even more immediately interested in their claims to total authority within the societies which they control. Both are still ardently interested in extending their authority over areas of the world where their national interests in the tangible sense are not immediately involved. Finally, both attempt to assert their authority over Communist parties both within and outside the bloc. To the extent that this authority is not based on the opportunity to exercise direct coercion, it must rest on the myth of the Communist Party. Essentially, the myth involves the ascription to the Communist Party—conceived of as the total world Communist movement—of all these transcendental and messianic qualities attributed by conventional Marxism to the world proletariat. The proletariat is an international class and its mission is a universal world historic mission. Only the proletariat can achieve socialism and communism. The proletariat is the first class in human history destined to confront the Truth about man and the world without beclouding delusions. "The proletariat cannot abolish itself without the realization of philosophy." Since the Truth is one, it follows that the proletariat is held together by an undivided general will. It is a class held together in iron unity by a kind of preestablished harmony. To these notions, the myth of the Communist Party adds the further notion that all of the attributes of the proletariat become incarnate in the Communist Party or, rather, in the present leader or leadership of the Communist Party, for the fact is that, in tracing the origins of this development, one must begin not with the Communist Party but with the person of Lenin. What we have at the outset is Lenin's own burning conviction that he and only he understands the general will of the Russian proletariat. The emergence of the Communist Party may be considered a result of the groping effort to embody this personal charisma within an institution or "church."

It must also be added that Lenin—and the Communist Party after him—makes a kind of truth claim for the proletariat which goes beyond the truth claim of earlier Marxism which stresses the grasp of certain large fundamental truths about the nature of man and the world. In fact, Lenin negates the assumption that the unfolding flux of political events can be simply deduced from the larger framework of Marxist truth. He negates the view that the road ahead is clearly discernible. On the contrary, reality is rich in unforeseen twists and turns, and only the proletariat—or rather its vanguard—can know how to apply the larger universal truths to unforeseen emergent situations. In the words of Stalin, theory provided "the right orientation in any situation" and makes it possible "to understand the inner connection of current events and to foresee their future course." The latter remark would seem to imply that theory applied to action or "party line" projects the future as well as describes the present. Thus, Lenin's "Democratic Dictatorship of the Workers and Peasants" was a theory designed to project the future as well as to describe the present. Yet, when the same Lenin boldly upset his own projection in 1917 on the ground that "life's green tree" had given rise to a new and unanticipated situation, he presumably lost none of his proletarian infallibility, for the fountainhead of the truth was to be sought not so much in the previous theory as in Lenin himself or in the party leadership which succeeded him. The Communist Party, thus, has the unique power to proclaim absolute truths concerning the unfolding flux of world events. The truths themselves may change with every shift in circumstance, but their validity is beyond question so long as they are promulgated by the vanguard of the proletariat.

Not only may the truth shift in time, it may also vary in space. It was, of course, Lenin himself who proclaimed the notion of "many paths to socialism," contrary to certain stereotypes. Stalin also paid due respect to this doctrine. It was, indeed, his claim that he had himself discovered the peculiarities and particularities of the Chinese revolution and prescribed the strategy appropriate to that revolution. After World War II, the notion of "people's democracy" was credited to Stalin as an alternate path to socialism appropriate to Eastern Europe. It is true that running counter to this tendency to acknowledge variant paths to socialism one finds a strong opposing tendency to stress the universal relevance of one's own model. After the Tito crisis, the slogan of variant paths to socialism swiftly gave way to the slogan that the model of people's democracy was, in essence, the same as the model of the Soviet Union. The Chinese Communists who have constantly stressed the particularity of their path to socialism incessantly stress the universal applicability of their own model to Asian, African, and Latin American conditions. However, whether the stress is on variation or on the universal model, the crux of the matter is that it is the exclusive prerogative of the leadership of the world Communist movement to decide these matters. It is not a question of whether variant paths to socialism are possible. It is a question of who promulgates and sanctions these paths. Furthermore, the authority to apply doctrine infallibly in time and space also involves the most awesome power of all—the power to decide which of the accepted "changeless and universal truths of Marxism-Leninism" may be rendered relative or superannuated by a "creative" application of doctrine.

The history of Communism has often been compared to the history of the church. Such comparisons may be illuminating so long as one bears in mind the differences in the specific doctrine of given churches. No church which has ever existed has enjoyed the "truth-making" powers of the Communist Party. Not only does it promulgate absolute truths concerning the flow of contingent events, it also possesses the power to change apparently unchanging and universal dogmas at will. Looking back from Marx to Hegel, one may say that the party itself embodies the *Weltgeist* as it manifests itself in the course of human history.

The grounds on which the Communist Party has claimed proletarian authority have, of course, changed and grown more attenuated over time. Contrary to frequent assertions,

Lenin was, on the whole, vitally interested in maintaining a tangible connection with the industrial proletariat. Even today, where the party actually enjoys an industrial proletarian base, as in France and Italy, there is a tendency in the Soviet Union to make much of this fact. It was, however, the Chinese experience, with its absolute divorce of the party from any tangible connection with the industrial proletariat, which led to the Chinese doctrine that the Communist Party in itself embodies what might be called the spiritual essence of the proletariat—an essence no longer dependent in any way on the social composition of the party or on any connection with the class. Where the Communist Party of the Soviet Union has found it to its advantage, it has also occasionally appropriated this doctrine to its own uses. Whatever the grounds on which this authority is claimed, however, both the Chinese and Russian parties still cling convulsively to the attributes of authority which they derive from the myth of the Communist Party. The Chinese party has, under the leadership of Mao, tended to combine this myth with formulas which allow a maximum appeal to populist-nationalist sentiment. Mao Tse-tung may incarnate "proletarian internationalism," but he is also the incarnation of the will of the Chinese people, and, in the image which it projects to the "third world," the Chinese Communist Party has in fact tended to stress the high degree of tolerance allowed by "the teachings of Mao Tsetung" to populist-nationalist sentiment. Nevertheless, the Chinese Communist Party has shown no inclination whatever to relinquish the type of transcendental authority which it derives from the myth of the Communist Party.

Internal Contradiction. If the myth of the Communist Party remains the vital core of Communism, it is a myth which—to borrow a phrase from the Communists—bears an internal contradiction at its very heart. The infallibility and monolithic unity presupposed in the myth can be maintained only so long as the party speaks with one voice, so long as there is an unquestioned ultimate instance of authority. When the Communist International was formed, Lenin did not plan in any premeditated fashion to impose the authority of the Russian party on the world movement. Yet, his own conviction that there was only one correct proletarian line for, let us say, the German and Italian proletariat, the assurance with which he lectured the Germans on their infantilism and the Italians on their manifold errors, inexorably extended to the world proletariat the type of authority which Lenin had already come to claim for himself vis-à-vis the Russian proletariat. Omniscience was implicit in his whole outlook, and, here again, the institution becomes an extension of the man. In fact, Lenin was able, up to a point, to maintain the unquestioned authority of the Communist Party of the Soviet Union within the international Communist world by the sheer power of his spiritual influence. Stalin, who, of course, lacked this charisma, also conspicuously lacked the faith in intangible methods of maintaining authority. The infallible and unquestioned authority of the center was to be maintained where possible by direct administrative and coercive methods. Stalin was probably correct in his assumption that the kind of authority claimed by Moscow could be maintained only by such methods.

It is interesting to note in this connection the dilemmas of Trotsky and other oppositionists during the twenties. Trotsky was fervently convinced of his own rightness but fervently committed to the party myth. The center of authority in the party had, however, been captured by Stalin, and the tortured question arose as to how one could be right *against the party?* This dilemma was finally resolved by the establishment of the Fourth International, which was, however, unable to challenge Stalin's possession of

Leninist authority. Authority flourishes best where it is nourished by power.

Within this context, the assumption by Mao Tse-tung in the early forties of the authority to apply the "universal truths of Marxism-Leninism" to the particular situation of China marks a most important point in the church history of Communism. Behind it lie such factors as Mao's achievement of effective control of the Chinese Communist Party, the clear emergence of Chinese nationalism within the Chinese Communist movement, and Mao's own *hubris* as the great leader based, no doubt, on the genuine belief that he understood matters in China better than the men in the Kremlin. While the factor of Chinese nationalism is undoubtedly of primary importance, it must nevertheless be noted that Mao's gesture simultaneously—and paradoxically—involved a reaffirmation of the myth of the Communist Party. Precisely because Mao was now arrogating to himself a portion of the authority sanctioned by the myth of the Communist Party, it was more necessary than ever to reaffirm the bases of this authority. His famous pronouncements—and those of his co-theorist Liu Shao-ch'i—on "thought remolding" do, in fact, forcefully restate the whole myth in Chinese terms.

Mao had, to be sure, claimed only a portion of the world Communist movement's authority—that is, the authority to apply the universal truths of Marxism-Leninism to China's situation. There was no challenge to Stalin's ultimate authority in the world Communist movement at large, and presumably Mao's "creative extension" of Marxism-Leninism-Stalinism was in complete harmony with what had gone before. There is little reason to believe, however, that Stalin ever accepted his claim, and all Soviet accounts of the Chinese Communist victory until Stalin's death treat that victory as the result of Mao's successful implementation of Stalin's theories on the nature of the Chinese revolution.

Nevertheless, Stalin's unfortunate experience in Yugoslavia may have led to a certain caution in dealing with the Chinese even though both the Yugoslav and Chinese cases actually lent weight to his view that the authority of Moscow was safe only where local parties were directly and tangibly controlled from the center. Certainly, his behavior in Eastern Europe, where he did enjoy tangible control, gives ample evidence that he had not changed his basic approach where he felt that he could safely apply it.

The era of Khrushchev and of the Twentieth Party Congress of the Communist Party of the Soviet Union undoubtedly mark a new turning point in the attitude toward the exercise of authority. Just as Khrushchev seems to have truly believed that the fundamental authority of the party could be maintained within the Soviet Union with a reduction of terror, he seems also to have been optimistic about the possibility of maintaining Moscow's authority within the bloc with a minimum of coercive control. After all, Communist parties shared certain fundamental universal doctrines. The reiteration at the Twentieth Congress of the doctrine of varied paths to socialism by no means implied a renunciation of Moscow's authority in sanctioning such paths. Yet the paths which had been independently pursued by China and Yugoslavia—after 1948—were given a kind of limited ex post facto ratification, probably in the hope that all further elaborations of paths to socialism would be made with due regard for Moscow's authority.

The Chinese, on their side, welcomed the loosening of Moscow's authority, whatever their misgivings regarding the secret speech on Stalin. Like Khrushchev, they probably genuinely believed that the consensus required by the party myth could be maintained even with some dispersion of party authority. The ideological autonomy of the Chinese Communist movement was now openly proclaimed, and, in fact, in 1956–1957 the Chinese proceeded to elaborate a new "creative extension" of Marxism-Leninism in the so-called Hundred Flowers movement. There is no evidence that this movement was ratified by Moscow. On the contrary, whatever meager evidence we have would indicate as decided a lack of enthusiasm about such notions as "non-antagonistic contradictions among social classes" within socialist society as was later to be manifested toward the whole commune experiment. On the other hand, the East European "liberals" drew considerable aid and comfort from the Hundred Flowers slogan. At the present time, when there is a widespread supposition that Sino-Soviet differences hinge solely on the question of Chinese "hardness" and Soviet "moderation," it is well to remind ourselves that, as recently as 1956–1957, the Chinese were, in Eastern Europe, the symbol of a flexible "creative" approach while Khrushchev was the defender of orthodoxy. If Khrushchev's experience in Eastern Europe during the latter months of 1956 brought him sharp disappointments, his experience with China probably convinced him that China remained a separate, incalculable entity not amenable to Soviet authority either in its domestic or foreign policies.

Authority. I shall not enter here into a detailed discussion of the substantive issues which have emerged between the Soviet Union and China since 1957. The issues of the "communes," of coexistence, and of policy vis-à-vis the nonaligned world have been quite adequately covered elsewhere—for example, in Donald S. Zagoria's book, *The Sino-Soviet Conflict.*[1] I shall, rather, focus briefly on the question of authority which is deeply involved with and yet may override the substantive issues. While the substantive issues—particularly the differing postures on the question of coexistence—are real enough, shifts of position on both

[1] *The Sino-Soviet Conflict, 1956–1961* (Princeton: Princeton University Press, 1962).

sides can by no means be precluded, and it is precisely here that overly "profound" explanations of the current substantive issues in terms of culture, history, and sociology may lead us to attribute a fixity to these positions which may not be warranted. There have, in fact, been actual marked oscillations in both the Chinese and Soviet lines toward the nonaligned world, which has so far failed, on the whole, to respond to the expectations of either. The Chinese have not found the emergence of broad revolutionary united fronts under Communist Party leadership. In the absence of the desired model, they have, on the one hand, enthusiastically supported revolution everywhere, Communist-led or otherwise, and, on the other, maintained good relations with established "bourgeois" (in their sense) regimes where it has suited their purpose. The Soviets have so far had reason to be disappointed in their expectations that "national democracy" would necessarily provide favorable "objective conditions" for the activities of Communist parties. On the one hand, they have continued to support these regimes. On the other, they have talked more and more insistently about the necessity of supporting and fostering independent Communist parties in these areas.

Cutting through all substantive issues, the crisis of authority has deepened progressively over time. In November 1957, on the occasion of Mao's visit to Moscow, we seem to have a paradoxical situation in which Mao Tse-tung insists on Moscow's central position in the bloc even while Khrushchev disavows the "need for a center which would guide the Communist movement." [2] The reality is much more complex. The late 1956 events in the bloc as well as domestic events in China had, to be sure, strongly reinforced Mao's own realization that the myth of the Communist Party requires an ultimate unchallengeable instance of authority.

[2] Interview with Henry Shapiro cited in Zagoria, *The Sino-Soviet Conflict,* p. 147.

The very context, however, in which Mao announced the fact that "the socialist camp must have a head" actually gives evidence of new pretensions to authority on the part of the Chinese Communist Party. It is in his speech in Moscow that Mao assumes the mantle of co-creator of policy for the Communist bloc as a whole. If Moscow was to remain the symbolic center of authority, Moscow should henceforth make bloc policy with the sanction of Peking. On the other hand, Khrushchev's disavowal of Moscow's pretensions to lead the bloc—disavowals which have been repeated over and over in many varying formulas—represent not a real renunciation of Moscow's central authority but rather a continued effort to avoid the appearance of Stalinist domination. It is not that Moscow insists on its own leadership. It is rather that all Communist parties naturally look to Moscow as the historically destined center of authority. If proletarian unity is to be based on the correct Marxist-Leninist line, who is to determine this line? If all watches are to be synchronized, on whose watch shall they be synchronized? Khrushchev modestly abstains from pressing Moscow's authority. Yet the meetings of the various national party congresses at the end of 1962 "naturally" recognized the Soviet position as the "rallying center of all the forces fighting for national independence, peace, democracy and socialism." [3] It is, of course, true that, with the decline of Moscow's authority, "polycentrism" has indeed become an emerging reality. It would be a grievous mistake to suppose, however, that it is a reality in any way welcomed by the Soviet leadership.

It might be asked again, however—why can a basic unity not be achieved within the Communist world on a kind of "federal" basis? The conference of 1957 did actually establish a kind of minimum Communist credo agreed upon by

[3] "Cementing the Unity of the Communist Movement is our International Duty," *World Marxist Review*, Feb. 1963, p. 4.

both the Chinese and the Soviets designed to separate Marx-ist-Leninist goats from all the sheep outside. As we know, however, this credo, which is still accepted by both sides, has not prevented a further deterioration of authority, because both the Chinese and Soviets have ever since claimed for themselves the full authority conferred by the myth of the Communist Party. The Soviets have exercised their pre-rogative to make a "creative" revision of Leninism. To the Chinese, they have violated one of the "universal truths of Marxism-Leninism." In 1958 the Chinese Communists pre-sumed to create their own definition of the prerequisites of the Communist stage of society—a definition which the So-viets could hardly ignore, for they have been busily engaged in fashioning their own definition, and, on this matter, the Russians are the more orthodox. The Chinese have pre-sumed to question the right of the Soviet Union to eject the Albanian party from the fold and have, since 1960, put forth the striking thesis that "no one has the right to de-mand that all fraternal parties should accept the theses of any one Party." This plea for absolute equality is, however, simultaneously accompanied by the constant assertion that only the Chinese party has correctly interpreted Marxism-Leninism.

It is still not impossible that the Communist world may again reestablish a kind of precarious solidarity on the basis of some kind of Communist parliamentarianism. Such soli-darity can be achieved, however, only at the expense of the myth of the Communist Party. It will have to be recognized that the "world proletariat" may speak with many voices on the same issue, that, contrary to Chou En-lai's formula at the Twenty-second Congress, the monolithic unanimity of the "world proletariat" can hardly be achieved by consulta-tion. It will finally have to be recognized that sectors of the proletariat which persist in their "wrong" views can no longer be relegated to the limbo of anti-Leninism. A "world

147

proletariat" which behaves in this way is hardly the "world proletariat" which figures in the party myth. To achieve solidarity on such a basis may indeed be too high a price to pay, for the myth remains of vital importance to both Chinese and Soviets in terms of the authority of the leadership within their own societies.

Viewing the whole development from the outside, it seems to me that the weakening of this central myth of Marxism-Leninism can only be regarded as a most welcome development. It does not necessarily imply the weakening of either Communist China or the Soviet Union as world states, but it does strengthen the hope of the possible emergence of international relations in which the role of absolutist political ideology may be reduced. Whether the United States government can do very much to effect this development is perhaps doubtful, but it can be alert to the emergence of all sorts of new possibilities. In facing these possibilities, it would again be well to bear in mind that the crisis in the Communist world does not merely revolve around China's "toughness" and the Soviet Union's "moderation," both of which are probably subject to change, but around an issue which is probably even more fundamental —the question of whether the myth of the Communist Party is any longer viable.

6

SOME COMMENTS ON SINO-SOVIET POLEMICS (1964)

Mao Tse-tung and his ideological experts are, as we know, earnest supporters of the Marxist-Leninist view that human nature "is determined by class origin." Indeed, one of the numerous and erroneous charges hurled from Peking at the Soviet leaders is that the latter have become partisans of the concept of a universal human nature. The Chinese, on the other hand, presumably cling to the absolute metaphysical concept of class nature, which assigns to men of different classes entirely different characteristics. The Chinese Communist Party, however shaky its credentials, is presumably the embodiment of the class nature of the international proletariat.

It is noteworthy that in all the discussions on this subject, the Chinese always seem to assume that the universal human nature, if it existed, would be a good, an ideal human

NOTE: This essay was first published under the title "The Polemics Seen by a Non-Polemicist" in *Problems of Communism*, March-April 1964.

149

nature. This, of course, may be a tribute to the dominant role of Mencius in Chinese Confucianism. The thought that what men share in common might be their *misère*—their frailties, deceptions, and vanities—as much as their *grandeur* does not seem to arise. Unfortunately for this dogma, the growing volume of Sino-Soviet polemic provides a mountain of evidence that if there is a common human nature, its denominator may be man's wretchedness. The record of the dispute is *allzu menschlich*. The ploys, evasions, prevarications, distortions, and self-pleading are quite comprehensible in terms of any heated argument between two "bourgeois" housewives screaming at each other over the back fence—in spite of the enormous machinery of Marxist-Leninist terminology.

In the following pages I should like to deal with certain developments in the polemic with a particular focus on the Chinese side. Somehow there is a general impression that the Chinese disputants are more "orthodox" and consistent, "purer," less "commonly human" in the various ways mentioned above than their Soviet antagonists. This impression is somewhat doubtful.

There is, to be sure, one issue on which the Chinese seem to be clearly on the side of orthodoxy, namely, "the question of war and peace." Yet even here all is not as clear as it appears. It is true, of course, that the Soviet Union and Communist China have adopted different foreign policy postures vis-à-vis the United States, but when we consider the theoretical question of "coexistence" as understood by Lenin complications arise. There is one locus classicus for Lenin's views on coexistence and world war which runs: "The existence of the Soviet Republic side by side with imperialist states for a long time is unthinkable . . . One must triumph in the end, and before that end supervenes, a series of frightful collisions between the Soviet Republic and the bourgeois states will be inevitable." [1]

Here we have an unqualified prediction of world wars. Most other pronouncements on coexistence can be reinterpreted to fit Soviet needs, but a statement of this kind from the Soviet point of view requires the application of "Marxist-Leninist creativity."

How have the Chinese interpreted this statement? They have occasionally cited it, as in the article on "Two Diametrically Opposed Policies of Coexistence," [2] to project an image of the "imperialists" much like the one in Lenin's statement. The "imperialists," it is implied, are like lemmings rushing toward the sea. They cannot help but make war. In actuality, however, the Chinese do not seem to have accepted the clear meaning of Lenin's assertion. Mao has, to be sure, deprecated the horrors of a nuclear war and indulged in his ghastly "socialist optimism" concerning the glories of the postwar period. But the fact remains that the Chinese have retreated from adopting publicly the plain meaning of the Leninist formula for obvious reasons of public relations if not from a genuine desire to avoid the holocaust. Also, while their image of the "imperialists" seems to be that of the lemmings, it is in fact somewhat more complicated.

Why "war maniacs" with nuclear weapons in both hands should refrain from using them when threatened with extinction is somewhat of a puzzle. Yet the Chinese continue to insist that war is not inevitable, provided that the "correct" approach prevails. Even while minimizing the effects of a new world war, Mao is also quoted as saying in Moscow

[1] Report of the Central Committee of the Russian Communist Party at the Eighth Party Congress. V. I. Lenin, *Selected Works* (Moscow, 1952), vol. 18, p. 33.

[2] *Peking Review,* Dec. 25, 1963.

in 1957 that "the East Wind prevails over the West Wind and that war will not break out." [3] The Chinese view, therefore, is that if the "imperialists" can be intimidated and thrown off guard by a steady stream of "national liberation wars" and "people's revolutionary struggles," they will ignominiously shrink to nothingness without ever flinging their bombs. The "imperialists" are, after all, capable of being paralyzed with fear and vacillation, and this may be sufficient to inhibit the remorseless workings of the "imperialist system." All that the Soviet position adds to this is the notion that in addition to their capacity for fear, the "imperialists" may also be capable of sober calculation.

It is, of course, possible that this is merely a tactical exoteric doctrine, while the esoteric doctrine remains the one outlined in Lenin's statement. It is nevertheless the exoteric doctrine which is being paraded by the Chinese as genuine Marxism-Leninism, and as such it remains a retreat from Lenin's unqualified prediction. As Mencius pointed out long ago, he who retreats fifty paces has little cause to laugh at him who retreats one hundred.

The Soviet side freely admits that Khrushchev has modified Lenin's position on this matter and simply claims that it has creatively applied Leninism to a new, unanticipated situation. Such "creative applications" of Marxism-Leninism have been the prerogative of the CPSU ever since Lenin began indulging in *his* "creative applications" of Marxism. We are all familiar by now with Mao Tse-tung's numerous claims to "creative applications" of Marxist-Leninist-Stalinist truth in all of which the same procedure is invariably involved. What had previously been considered a universal truth—a proposition applying to all places and all times in modern history—is suddenly relativized and limited in applicability to certain places and certain limited segments of

[3] Statement by the spokesman of the Chinese Government, in *Peking Review*, Sept. 6, 1963, p. 10.

time. Lenin's doctrines concerning the inevitability of world wars, state the Soviet theoreticians, were true only for the period of time preceding the emergence of nuclear military technology. According to China's ideological spokesman, Chou Yang, however: "The leaders of the CPSU who boast of having developed Marxism-Leninism in a creative manner permit themselves and their followers to revise Marxism-Leninism while they try to prevent others from developing it in a truly creative fashion . . . Even while adulterating Marxism-Leninism at their own discretion, they demand that the other Communist parties follow their steps and repeat their words as if their adulteration were an imperial edict." [4]

The guileless Chou Yang is evidently unaware that during the long reign of Stalin Moscow's claims to creativity *were* "imperial edicts" based ultimately on an assumption of superior authority.

What, then, about Mao Tse-tung's claims to creativity? Can one really find in the copies of Lenin's and Stalin's writings proof texts for all of Mao's "innovations"? To take one of the most recent themes of Chinese propaganda, what would Lenin have made of a socialist world made up of sovereign nation-states, each developing its own economy in complete "self-reliance" and autarchy? The reasons for Peking's adoption of this bit of "creativity" are obvious, but whether Lenin would have considered it more "creative" than Moscow's position on coexistence is open to question. Both the Chinese and Soviets, of course, appeal to "life" to verify their respective "creative applications" of Marxism-Leninism, and "life" obligingly tells both of them exactly what they want to hear.

Turning from "the question of peace and war" to the question of ideological policy vis-à-vis the nonaligned world, we

[4] *Peking Review,* Jan. 3, 1964, p. 22.

find a very muddy picture indeed. The notion of a consistent Chinese posture in this area will hardly bear close scrutiny. During the period of the Chinese rise to power—roughly from 1948 to 1954—both Moscow and Peking seemed to be equally hostile to the newly emerging "bourgeois nationalist" regimes in Asia and equally inclined to dismiss them as lackeys of imperialism. There was a similar tendency to favor only nationalist movements under Communist party control. Liu Shao-ch'i, now chief of state, proclaimed in his famous speech to the WFTU in 1949 the universal validity of the Chinese model with respect to seizure of power in colonial and semicolonial areas, including all the specifications—the broad united front under "proletarian hegemony," the possession of a revolutionary army, armed revolution against armed counterrevolution, and so forth.[5] The Soviets, however, did not commit themselves to the particulars of the Chinese model and preferred to stress their own favorite category of "people's democracy." Peking's insinuation that China had a particular message for the Asian, African, and Latin American world over and above the message of the October Revolution was never accepted. Nevertheless, both sides shared the doctrine that national liberation movements everywhere should be controlled by Communist parties.

In the period 1950–1955, however, we see on both sides a gradual drift from this approach to what became known as the Bandung line. With the death of Stalin, the end of the Korean War, the rapid unanticipated retreat of colonial power, and the rise of numerous non-Communist nation-states, both the new Soviet leadership and the Chinese found it in their interest to cultivate the new neutralist regimes and to acknowledge their independence in spite of the lack of "proletarian hegemony" anywhere in the ex-co-

[5] New China News Agency, Nov. 23, 1949.

lonial world. To be sure, both Moscow and Peking continued to cherish the hope of "proletarian hegemony" in the future, but during the whole period from 1955 to 1959 Peking was quite willing to push its previous doctrine of the universal relevance of the Chinese model into the background and to indulge in ardent wooing of all the established regimes in Asia, Africa, and elsewhere. Even at this time, incidentally, in spite of the common direction of Soviet and Chinese lines, there were numerous indications of tension between Peking and Moscow in the underdeveloped world. The famous trip of Bulganin and Khrushchev to Asia would seem to indicate that the Soviets were already deeply suspicious of what they now call Peking's "hegemonistic" pretensions in Asia, Africa, and Latin America. Even at that point, a common ideological-strategic line was no guarantee against a silent struggle for authority and power.

Soviet policy, on the whole, has remained faithful to the Bandung line ever since, in spite of all the disappointments. It is this line which has come to be enshrined in the Soviet doctrine of "national democracy." Genuinely independent nationalist governments, we now learn, may be created by the nationalist bourgeoisie, the petty bourgeoisie, and the peasantry without the presence of the proletariat represented by the Communist Party. The conditions in such a "national democracy" are, however, invariably interpreted as favorable to the future advent of "socialism" and eventually "communism." Contrary to Chinese assertions, the Soviets are by no means indifferent to future "proletarian hegemony" and are rather constantly on the lookout—as one can readily attest in such Soviet journals as *Narody Azii i Afriki* (The Peoples of Asia and Africa)—for the emergence of Communist parties (faithful to Moscow) in these areas. There is indeed some evidence that in Guinea the Soviet Union took rather too much initiative in pushing the cause of "proletarian hegemony." Nevertheless,

155

they have patiently continued to cultivate regimes, such as that of Abdul Nasser, which go on suppressing their own Communist movements and taking aid from neo-colonialists.

It is, indeed, the Chinese who began to depart from the Bandung line, particularly during 1959. Events on the Indian border, events in Iraq, and the policies of Nasser, as well as the atmosphere of Peking's internal policy, may all have played a part in this; whatever the reasons, the Chinese seemed to return to something like the pre-Bandung line. Presumably there was a renewed emphasis on proletarian hegemony within the national liberation movement, on broad united fronts of the "four classes" led by the Communists, on armed struggle, and so forth.

The word "presumably" must be stressed here, for in actuality Peking's ideological posture between 1959 and the end of 1963 remained somewhat muffled. It is true that in this period there were many treatises in Chinese journals dealing with the history of the CCP's rise to power and strongly implying the universal applicability of this experience to the whole non-Western world.[6] There is also considerable evidence that at the 1960 meeting of Communist parties in Moscow the Chinese strongly insisted on their own "principled" version of "national democracy," emphasizing the quick attainment of "proletarian hegemony," the turn away from the reactionary bourgeoisie in the new areas, and so on. Perhaps the clearest expression of the Chinese ideological posture in recent years was provided in the famous CCP letter of June 14, 1963, entitled "A Proposal Concerning the General Line of the International Communist Movement," which stated: "History has entrusted to the proletarian parties in these areas the glorious mission of

[6] For the most recent statement, see "The Victorious Road of National Liberation War," *Peking Review*, Nov. 15, 1963.

holding high the banner of struggle against imperialism
. . . of standing in the forefront of the national democratic
revolutionary movement and striving for a socialist future."

The fact remains, however, that in many of the new countries no "proletarian parties" existed and that Peking continued throughout the period to cultivate relations with
such countries. Not only did it continue to cultivate Ghana,
Guinea, and Mali, but also "feudal," royalist Yemen and
Nepal. In the case of the Algerian revolt, Peking constantly
stressed the "Chinese" nature of the strategy employed, in
spite of the fact that the revolution was by no means "under proletarian hegemony." There were sound "raisons
d'état" for these Chinese policies, but they by no means support Peking's claims of a "principled" ideological posture
totally differing from that of the Soviets.

Finally, the most recent development in Chinese policy has
been a second, quiet return to the Bandung line. Chou En-
lai's recent trip to Africa has given evidence of this new
shift in policy, not widely publicized abroad. Abdul Nasser,
who for a long time had been discreetly assigned by Peking
to the category of reactionary tools of imperialism, now
found himself praised by Chou for "successes in the defense
of his fatherland, state sovereignty, etc.," [7] in spite of his
continued suppression of the Egyptian Communist Party,
continued acceptance of "neo-colonialist" aid, and continued cordial relations with Tito. Bourguiba and the
King of Morocco were likewise congratulated on their genuine national independence. Peking is issuing invitations to
a new "Bandung" conference of all Asian, African, and
Latin American countries without regard to polity. The
only state which the Chinese now consider to have become
a reactionary bourgeois puppet of imperialism is Nehru's

[7] The China-UAR Joint Communique, *Peking Review*, Dec. 27, 1963,
p. 9.

India. Under these circumstances, it becomes increasingly difficult to define precisely what are the ideological differences between Moscow's conception of "national democracy" and Peking's. Their specific policies in specific areas (for example, India) may differ widely, and the "hegemonistic" rivalry between them is obvious; but the question of ideological principle has become completely befogged.

The Chinese have, in fact, now launched a major campaign to "unite with whom one can unite" on a global basis. This motto is now meant to include not merely classes and political groupings within given states, but whole nation-states regardless of their political and social systems. It is to include not only the first "intermediate zone" of Africa, Asia, and Latin America, but also, if possible, the "second intermediate zone" of the capitalist and even "imperialist" states of the West, excluding "U.S. Imperialism" which is now defined as the exclusive enemy (perhaps the Soviet Union is also excluded).[8] All of these forces may conceivably be united against "U.S. Imperialism"!

The Chinese motto of "uniting with whom one can unite" has always been coupled with the phrase "under the hegemony of the proletariat." It is only the combination of the two which constitutes Mao's "creative contribution to Marxism-Leninism." It is of course possible for the Chinese to believe that de Gaulle's recognition of Peking involves an acknowledgment of Peking's "proletarian hegemony," but it will hardly serve their purposes to inform the General of such a belief. And if they are attempting to stress a united front with Canada and France against the United States, they are not likely to press the issue. Such has been the "principled" history of Peking's ideological relations to the nonaligned world.

[8] "All the World's Forces Opposing U.S. Imperialism Unite," *Peking Review,* Jan. 24, 1964, pp. 6–8.

Unnoticed in the exchange of invective between Peking and Moscow, there has emerged yet one more creative addition to Marxism-Leninism which has quietly been accepted by both sides—probably in a more unqualified way by the Chinese than by the Soviets. It involves nothing less than a redefinition of the prerequisites for the existence of a Marxist-Leninist movement and is largely the result of Castro's self-definition as a Marxist-Leninist. When the famous credo of 1957 was drawn up—a credo to which both Moscow and Peking still fervently appeal—phrases such as "Marxist-Leninist parties," "Communist and workers' parties," "proletarian parties" were used interchangeably, and it would not have occurred to any of the signatories that these phrases might refer to different realities. Now we read the following in an interview granted by Chou En-lai to the Uruguayan journalist, Galeano, on December 13, 1963: "If a country wants to carry out a socialist revolution, it should accept the revolutionary principles of Marxism-Leninism, and Marxism-Leninism cannot be the monopoly of the Communist Party. Any revolutionary can use the weapon. When Fidel Castro achieved victory through armed combat, he was not a member of the Communist Party."[9]

In other words, we now learn that Marxism-Leninism is separable from those determined entities known as Communist parties, and that political groups and political leaders clearly not committed to Marxism-Leninism, and hence clearly not "proletarian," may, by a process of self-definition, become genuinely Marxist-Leninist. Further, since all political groups and parties by Communist definition represent classes, one must assume that political groups which do not represent the proletariat must obviously represent some nonproletarian class—that is, the national bourgeoisie,

[9] JPRS Translations on International Communist Developments, Washington, D.C., no. 552, Jan. 20, 1964.

the petty bourgeoisie, the peasantry, and so forth. Now, some of these political groups are informed that they may transform their "class nature" simply by a process of self-definition.

In his speech in Algeria, we find that Chou lavished extravagant praise on Algeria's "revolutionary" road to freedom, its "armed struggle," and the like: "The independence of Algeria in our era is a great event in the African national liberation movement. For the other African peoples it has set a brilliant example of daring to wage an armed struggle and daring to seize victory and indicates to the oppressed nations throughout the world *the correct road to win independence and freedom.*" [10] I have emphasized the last phrase since it seems to be in flagrant contradiction to Chou's assurance to other nations in Africa which have won their independence by less spectacular methods that China fully accepts the reality of their national independence. But what is most remarkable in Chou's speech is the enormous emphasis placed on the parallels between the Chinese and Algerian revolutions. The only missing ingredient—an ingredient once considered the most essential of all—is the hegemony of a Marxist-Leninist party. The whole speech thus seems to represent a plea to Ben Bella to "do a Castro" and define his movement as a Marxist-Leninist movement. If Ben Bella makes the proper decision, his petty-bourgeois FLN will be transformed into the vanguard of the proletariat, while the CPSU, after forty years of Leninist steeling and tempering, sinks into bourgeois degeneration. Of course, the Marxism-Leninism to which "revolutionary groups" should commit themselves is only genuine Marxism-Leninism, and everyone knows that precious commodity is dispensed only in Peking.

Thus, the essence of the true proletarian class nature is now not only detached from the industrial proletariat, it

[10] *Peking Review,* Jan. 3, 1964, p. 34. Italics added.

is even detachable from constituted Communist parties. It is now a completely free-floating fluid which may find its embodiment where it listeth.

This essay has focused on Chinese manipulation of ideology because of the widespread impression that the Chinese have been less cavalier and more rigidly doctrinaire than the Soviets in their ideological stance. On the whole, it is true that they have attempted to give an impression of greater toughness, but toughness has no necessary relationship to rigidity. In none of this do I mean to imply that the Soviet side of the controversy will bear close scrutiny.

Contrary to Soviet assertions, as already pointed out, the Chinese have not clearly committed themselves to world war, nor have they in any of their public statements emphasized color or race. The Chinese also seem quite correct, it seems to me, in their claim that the Soviets still clearly aspire to "wave the baton" in the Communist world in spite of their frequent protestations that there is no longer any "center" in that world. The Soviet claim to ascendancy now simply takes the form of alleging the "unanimity" of all Communist parties in accepting the decisions of all recent Soviet party congresses as binding upon all of them. It is precisely the Chinese refusal to accept the binding nature of these decisions that has shaken the whole structure of authority in the Communist world to its very foundations.

7

MODERNIZATION AND THE MAOIST VISION: SOME REFLECTIONS ON CHINESE COMMUNIST GOALS (1965)

What can be said at this point about the broad goals and motivations of the present Chinese Communist leadership? The question is, of course, distressingly imprecise and begs further definition. Is the leadership a monolithic group? Have its goals remained constant and unchanging? Is there a rigid Chinese Communist "goal structure," and so forth?

On the question of leadership I shall simply adhere to the conventional hypothesis that Mao Tse-tung and those closest to him have played a leading role in determining basic policy shifts during the last fifteen years. There may have been moments when his presence has receded from the center of the stage. In the early years after 1950, his role may have been somewhat inhibited by the awesome presence of Stalin. His influence may have flagged at the Wuhan meeting at the end of 1958 and after the retreat from the "Great

NOTE: This essay was first published in *The China Quarterly*, January-March 1965.

Leap Forward." On the whole, however, óne perceives the imprint of his outlook (probably developed in close collaboration with Liu Shao-ch'i) at almost every crucial turning point from the land reform campaign of 1950 to the present frenzied drive for "socialist education."

On the matter of goals, while there is certainly no rigid static "goal structure," while the relationship among goals has undoubtedly been enormously complex, problematic, and shifting over time, it may nevertheless be possible to speak of a certain range of broad goals which has remained fairly constant and which may have set certain outer limits to the possibilities of policy choice. This does not mean, one should hasten to add, that the whole history of Communist China during the last fifteen years can be understood in terms of an unproblematic implementation of the leadership's goals. Unyielding objective conditions, unforeseen events and contingencies, and the recalcitrances of human nature have certainly been just as decisive as the goals of the leadership in shaping the history of China since 1949. Interpretations of events in Communist China have often swung wildly from the view that China is an inert clay in the hands of the leaders who shape it as they will to the view that everything that has happened is a result of an iron "objective necessity" which shapes all the leadership's decisions. All that will be urged in this essay is that the goals of the leadership have been one of the factors shaping the course of events.

There has been much discussion of Chinese Communist goals during the last decade and a half and there is a certain range of broad assumptions which can be discerned in most analyses of the Chinese scene whether written by academic experts poring over Chinese Communist media or visitors who have been there. One such widely shared assumption is that the overriding, indeed, all-embracing goal of the Chinese Communist leadership is to achieve the modernization of China or—put somewhat differently—everything that is happening in Communist China is an aspect of the process of modernization. There is also the assumption that the basic goal of the leadership is the achievement of a certain vision of society spelled out in the scriptures of Marxism-Leninism-Maoism. This vision may involve aspects of what is called "modernization" in the West, but modernization is conceived of as a part of a much larger whole defined by the ideology. This view of the goals of the leadership is, of course, the avowed view of the leadership itself, but it is also shared by many others who may be ardently attracted to the vision or violently repelled by it. Another view places central stress on nationalism—on the goal of national power and prestige and on the achievement of world power status as quickly as possible. It is of course true that to the protagonists of the modernization school nationalism is simply an "aspect" or "function" of some all-inclusive modernization process and hence not to be considered under a separate rubric. To others it must be considered as a force in its own right. There is another view which may be said to concern motivation more than goals—namely, that the Chinese Communist leadership is essentially engrossed in the limitless "totalitarian" aggrandizement of its own power, both within China and in the world at large. There are undoubtedly other assumptions which can and have been made concerning the goals and motives of the leaders, but I shall confine my attention to these.

Power. Turning first of all to the view that all the policies and decisions of the leadership are designed to maximize its power, we find that in recent years, particularly since the death of Stalin, there has been a distinct decline in the popularity of the "theory of totalitarianism" or all theories which stress the power drives of the leadership. There has, in fact, been a tendency on the part of some to brush aside

164

the relevance of power considerations entirely on grounds which are a shade too facile. Power, we are told, is not an end in itself. It is functional to goals which lie beyond it or it plays a certain function in the larger social system, and so on. It must always be explained in terms of "larger" social, historic, and economic forces of which it is the mere instrument. One might say that for the whole course of human history power has always been "functional." It has always led to objective results, bad or good, which have survived its pursuit. This is just as true of Rameses and Ch'in Shih Huang-ti as it is of Mao Tse-tung. This by no means precludes the fact that it has also been pursued as an end in itself and that this pursuit has played its own role in human history. "Objectively" Macbeth may have been a most successful Scottish "state-builder," but this by no means proves that the side of him which Shakespeare chooses to depict is irrelevant to a discussion of his day-to-day political behavior. Power has always been functional and always been demonic and the end is not yet in sight. What vitiates the narrow "power approach" is the assumption that a concern with the maintenance or expansion of power is necessarily incompatible with the pursuit of more general goals. If the Chinese Communist Party is conceived of as the sole effective instrument for achieving a certain vision of the good society or for making China a great world power or for consummating the process of modernization, then the general goals and power considerations may actually reinforce and enhance each other.

Those who deny the relevance of power considerations might at this point maintain, however, that if power considerations and objective goals often move in the same direction why assign any particular causal weight to power considerations? In fact, however, at given points in time they may by no means move in the same direction. If one assumes that one of the basic domestic aims of the "Hundred Flowers" campaign was to give the intelligentsia (a term which, of course, includes professionals as well as academic and literary intellectuals) an opportunity to participate more fully and freely in the economic and scientific development of China; if a reasoned judgment had been made that further economic and scientific development required the more positive participation of the intelligentsia, one can hardly say that the experiment was given time to prove itself. The fact that Mao Tse-tung was still vigorously supporting the program in February 1957 only to allow himself to be won over to the opposition (which had undoubtedly been strong in the party from the outset) within the next few months can hardly be due to its failure to produce spectacular economic results in the early months of 1957. The drive was speedily terminated when it seemed to involve a threat to the unlimited political power of the leadership. Similarly, while the purges of Kao Kang and Jao Shu-shih in 1954 and of P'eng Teh-huai in 1959 undoubtedly involved policy differences from the outset, it is quite clear that in the end these "antiparty elements" were associated with a threat to power. The vehemence with which the ideological remolding of the army was carried on in the 1960–1962 period can hardly be disassociated from this threat to power.

All of these instances, of course, involve not so much a concern for the expansion of power as for the preservation of power in being, and it may well be one of the defects of the theory of totalitarianism that it dogmatically assumes that the concern for power must always be a concern for its maximization. It makes no allowance for the possibility that a concern for the maintenance of power in being may, at times, outweigh the concern for its maximization in the future. Nevertheless, the power approach reminds us that we are dealing with a group of men who know and savor power and its uses as much as any ruling group that has ever existed. They are not merely the embodiment of a social vision, or the destiny of China, or the process of modernization. Mao's spectacular projection of his own authority in the Communist bloc and the world at large and the present hysterical cult of Mao in China may serve a certain vision of the world or be in line with certain policies but also admirably feed his limitless *hubris*. The factor of power is relevant to a discussion of all these policies and shifts in policy. Indeed, at points where the implementation of policy may seem to endanger power interests, it may be the most relevant factor of all.

Modernization. If the ever-present concern with power by no means precludes the pursuit of broader goals—what are these broader goals? One widely accepted response is that the goal is the modernization of China. One could, of course, devote volumes to a discussion of the meaning of this term, and yet there does seem to be a kind of common core of shared meaning which is implicit at least in most American discussions. In general, it tends to mean something approximating Max Weber's conception of the process of rationalization in all those spheres of social action —economic, political, military, legal, educational—which lend themselves to the application of *"Zweckrationalität."* It involves the sustained attention to the most appropriate, "rational," and efficient methods for increasing man's ability to control nature and society for a variety of ends. Economists often treat it as being coextensive with industrialization, and it is indeed in this area that the meaning of the term "rationalization" can be most concretely elucidated. Weber himself in spite of his tendency to use the cover term "capitalism" (presumably an economic category) was just as much concerned with political bureaucracy, military development, and legal "rationalization." It tends to involve the notion of a highly developed division of labor

167

of "functional specificity" with the corollary that men should have a degree of autonomy and authority within their various areas of competence. It also involves a stress on norms of universality rather than ascription and, thus, should involve social mobility—the opening up of careers to talents. Looking at the whole concept from the point of view of China, one is inclined to stress that it also may involve a sober respect for objective conditions. The technician and, for that matter, the professional bureaucrat will be very conscious of the limits imposed by their materials and by the imperatives of the situation within which they operate.

Actually one can distinguish two versions of the concept of modernization which may have quite different implications. One version treats the "process of modernization" as a vast, indeed, an all-embracing impersonal historic force. Revolutions, ideologies, nationalism, and the policies of governments are all surface eruptions of this underlying process which is independent of the wills of men and operates behind their backs very much like Hegel's *"Weltgeist"* or Marx's "mode of production." In the other version, modernization becomes a conscious project or consciously entertained goal of large or small groups of men. The two versions may have quite different consequences for an analysis of the behavior of the Chinese leadership. If modernization is an all-enveloping force which controls all the acts both conscious and unconscious of the leadership, all their acts must be explained as a "function" of the modernization process. The leadership may explicitly profess concern with other matters; it may even sincerely be concerned "subjectively" with other matters. In fact, all its behavior is determined by the imperatives of the modernization process. If, on the other hand, modernization is a goal consciously pursued, it is not impossible that it may compete in the minds of the leadership with other goals. In fact, the decisions of the leadership may have something to do with shaping the order of priorities and strategies of the modernization process itself.

The adherents of the monistic modernization theory seldom, if ever, raise questions about the goals of modernization itself. It is assumed that the goals are immanent in the process and that we know what they are. Among many Americans there is in fact the latent assumption that a fully modernized society will look exactly like the United States with all its social and cultural specificities. Even if we assume that modernization is leading in the end of days to some universal homogenized human condition, *in processu* it is quite compatible with quite different conceptions of the priority of ends to be served. A highly advanced industrial society may be able to lavish equal resources on state power and prestige and welfare. A less developed society will have to make choices in this area and these choices may have a most profound effect on the strategy of modernization.

Nationalism. Viewed in this light nationalism may be much more than a "function" of the modernization process. Where it occupies a central place, it may actually determine the strategy of modernization. To assume that Stalin's lop-sided emphasis on heavy industrial development was a function of Soviet nationalism seems to make much more sense than to assume that it was the only rational strategy of industrialization in an underdeveloped area. Similarly one must assume that the apparent priority granted to nuclear development in China through all the recent shifts in economic strategy is related fundamentally to its nationalist goals rather than to any obvious imperative of the modernization process.

The Chinese leadership's unquestioning adoption of this model after 1950 was due not simply to the fact that it was the orthodox Marxist-Leninist model of economic development but also to the fact that Stalin had in this model already bent Marxism-Leninism to national power purposes. As perfervid Chinese nationalists, the Chinese leadership shared the preoccupations which lay behind Stalin's own choice of model. They were genuine Stalinists in their whole-hearted acceptance of Stalin's accommodation of Marxism-Leninism to the interests of a nation-state. It is thus entirely meaningful to stress that the speedy achievement of nationalist goals has been one of the unchanging central goals of the leadership which has shaped the priorities and strategy of the modernization process itself. This does not mean that the leadership is not committed to the welfare goals which we associate with modernization—with living standards, public health, literacy, and so on—but the relative priorities seem quite clear.

During the years from 1949–1956 there can be little doubt that the goal of modernization *on the Soviet model* was assiduously pursued by the Chinese Communist leadership in many sectors. After the Korean War we have a gradual implementation of the Soviet model of economic development. There is a movement towards the creation of a state structure with a modern bureaucratic apparatus and the professionalization of the army on a Soviet model is vigorously pursued. It has indeed become the tendency among some to regard this eminently Soviet phase of Chinese development as the "modernizing" phase par excellence as opposed to the irrationalities of subsequent phases. Yet, as we know, the relationship of the whole Soviet development to the supposed prerequisites of modernization has itself been the subject of endless, unresolved debates. Ideology is also deeply implicated in the whole Soviet development. What is mainly implied is that the Soviet model involves a stress on professionalization, on a degree of autonomy for professional hierarchies, particularly in the in-

170

dustrial, state administrative, and military spheres. Franz Schurmann has, for instance, stressed the emphasis during this period on the Soviet conception of managerial responsibility in industry (without necessarily regarding it as pre-eminently rational).

One of the most striking facts of recent Chinese Communist history (particularly since 1956) has been the gradual departure from the Soviet model of modernization. Some have leaped to the conclusion that this marks the departure from a "rational" approach to modernization. Yet it might well be argued that, in part, the departure from the Soviet model of modernization was due to the realization that this model was not applicable to China's real situation. The Chinese could not reduce the peasantry to a subsistence level and then ignore the agricultural sector. To keep their vast population alive at the barest subsistence level it became obvious that a maximum attention to agriculture was imperative. In the strictly economic sphere one might argue that the economic policy pursued after 1960 with its emphasis on "agriculture as the base" has been much more rational in terms of China's conditions than the model of the 1953–1956 period. In fact, one might argue that during the whole period from the "Hundred Flowers" campaign to the present campaign for "socialist education" all policies have borne some relationship to the problems of modernization.

The Maoist Vision of the Good Society. It nevertheless seems to me that if we are to understand some of the modes of response to these problems which have emerged since 1956, we must introduce another broad goal area which might be called ideological but which I shall refer to as the Maoist vision of the good society.

The vision involves not only a conception of the good society of the future but also a sanctified image of the

171

methods by which this vision is to be achieved. Certainly Marxist-Leninist-Stalinist ideology is one of the main sources of this vision, but this does not preclude the possibility that in some of its aspects it coincides with certain traditional Chinese habits of thought and behavior. It draws above all on the actual experience of the Communist movement during the thirties and forties, and the interpretation of this experience enshrined in the Yenan writings of Mao Tse-tung and Liu Shao-ch'i. As has often been pointed out, the "Yenan syndrome" seems to occupy a central, hallowed place in the vision of Mao Tse-tung, and most of the elements which form part of the Maoist vision first appear, at least in their embryonic form, during this period.

The phrase "Maoist vision" seems to describe a static frame of reference and almost suggests something like an "operational code" which may provide a key to all the shifts and twists of party policy since 1949. On the contrary, there is absolutely no reason to assume that it provided Mao with any prevision of the circumstances which were to give rise to the "Hundred Flowers" campaign or the "Great Leap Forward" campaign, or to the circumstances which were to lead to their abrupt demise. Not all elements of the vision have been equally prominent at all times and some of them have only been made fully explicit in the course of time. Many elements of the vision are highly ambivalent ("dialectic"), lending themselves to the support of quite opposing policies. And yet when viewed in the abstract, there is a kind of rough coherence among them.

Not only has the pursuit of this vision often cut across other goals of the leadership, but it has with varying degrees of intensity conditioned the manner in which these other goals have been pursued. Some elements of the vision have had an obvious and almost unremitting impact on reality. The enormous energies invested since 1949 in the effort to achieve the spiritual transformation of the entire Chinese people, whether in the form of "study" (*hsüeh-hsi*), "thought reform," "remolding," "education through labor," or "socialist education," is one of the most obvious instances. At another level, some elements of the vision have been invoked and made most explicit in connection with certain specific campaigns—such as the notion of "contradictions among the people" at the time of the "Hundred Flowers" campaign or the emphasis on "subjective forces," "revolutionary romanticism," and "man as the decisive factor" at the time of the "Great Leap Forward." One is tempted to say that, when invoked in this way, these ideological themes simply serve to confirm the infallibility of the "thought of Mao Tse-tung" in the face of all shifts and twists in line, and—particularly since 1956—to confirm ever more emphatically the autonomy and originality of the "Chinese path." Undoubtedly they do serve this purpose. Yet while these themes are hardly the "sufficient causes" of the campaigns of 1956, 1958, or other new departures, the genuine belief in the assumptions implicit in them may well explain the high confidence and élan with which these campaigns are pressed. One simply has to peruse Mao's comments in such works as *The Socialist Upsurge in China's Countryside* (1957) [1] to appreciate the fervor of his belief in those "facts" which seem to support his vision. At another level, however, elements of the vision are obviously manipulated simply as ideology in the narrowest sense. Thus the fact that the slogans of the "Hundred Flowers" movement and of the great leap continue to live on into periods when they no longer apply is obviously a device designed to prove that Mao's contributions to the

[1] Peking: Foreign Language Press.

storehouse of Marxism-Leninism are irrevocable and cumulative.

Consensus and Collectivism. What are some of the essential elements of the Maoist vision? There is first of all the overriding commitment to a society united by something approaching a total consensus and a society marked by radical collectivism. It may seem superfluous to speak of the collectivist goal of a Communist society, and yet the image of collectivity which has emerged in China, particularly since 1958, seems somewhat different in kind from that projected in the Soviet Union. The emphasis on the individual's total self-abnegation and total immersion in the collectivity as ultimate goods, the frequent reference to the model of military life with its nostalgic allusions to the heroic and idyllic guerrilla bands of the past are particular characteristics of the Maoist projection of the future. Lenin's own projection of Utopia in *State and Revolution* still draws heavily on Marx's own meager and vague descriptions which, as we know, speak in terms of the total liberation and self-fulfillment of the individual. Whether this language makes Marx a sort of ultimate liberal, as some of his interpreters would have us believe, may be open to serious doubt, yet there is the fact that the individual and his situation do play a central role in Marx's Utopia. While the Soviet official ideology has been as deeply suspicious of the whole notion of alienation in the young Marx as the Chinese, a somewhat crasser form of the concern with the interests of the individual can nevertheless be discerned in its projection of Communism. The Maoist version on the other hand projects a kind of collectivist mysticism. Commenting on the European and Soviet discussions of Marxism, Chou Yang states "that in advocating the return of Man to himself they are actually advocating absolute individual freedom and asking the people who live

under Socialism to return to the human nature of bourgeois individualism and to restore the capitalism by which
it is fostered." [2]

Even more characteristic has been the enormous emphasis
on the power of spiritual transformation (indoctrination
seems to be far too weak a term) to bring about this society
of collective man. The hope is that of a kind of total consensus achieved mainly by spiritual methods. The ultimate
roots of this emphasis may be sought in Lenin's own emphasis on the conscious factor (further extended by Stalin),
perhaps fed to some extent by the Confucian faith in the
power of moral influence. Its more immediate background
is to be sought in the circumstances of the Yenan period
when the methods of "remolding" were first applied to
members and prospective members of the Communist Party.
The notion was later vastly extended to include the whole
"people" including the "national bourgeoisie" however defined. The doctrine that all can be saved—even some "counterrevolutionary elements"—has, of course, always been
heavily qualified by the retention of the class notion. People of the wrong classes are not easily transformed, and
continue to generate poisons of wrong thought. Yet they
can be transformed while those of good class background
can be led astray. In the end the main criterion for assigning persons to the "people" or "nonpeople" is to be sought
in their spiritual attitudes rather than in the facts of their·
class origin. The doctrine of salvation stresses simultaneously that almost all men may be saved; that salvation is
enormously difficult for all men; and that backsliding is an
ever-present possibility. Paradoxically the emphasis on
spiritual transformation may lend itself to quite disparate
policies. The "Hundred Flowers" campaign may have been
predicated on the genuine belief that the intelligentsia had

[2] "Fighting Task of Workers in Philosophy and Social Science," *Peking Review,* Jan. 3, 1964.

been basically transformed during the 1949–1955 period, while the "Anti-rightist" campaign of 1957 was based on precisely the opposite assumption. The "Great Leap Forward" may have been based on the assumption that the "masses" (unlike the intelligentsia) had been basically transformed and that their "subjective forces" were at the disposal of the leadership, while the present campaign of "socialist education" seems to be predicated on the assumption that there is still much work to be done.

"Populism." The emphasis on spiritual transformation is closely linked to the "populist" theme. Because the whole people (defined as a union of four classes) can be transformed, the whole Chinese people can participate in the building of socialism and Communism. This doctrine finds its formal institutional expression in the coalition structure of government, and can, of course, be harnessed to the nationalist goals of the regime as well as to project the Chinese model to the "emerging world" where there is such an obvious political need to "unite with whom one can unite." The obverse side of the formula—the notion that the "people" is not homogeneous but composed of different classes which still engender "nonantagonistic" (and even antagonistic) contradictions—has, however, been of equal importance. It has justified the need for constant vigilance and unremitting indoctrination, but was also used to justify the vaguely defined legitimate area of "blooming and contending" of the "Hundred Flowers" period. On this side, it is particularly closely linked to another element of the Maoist vision, namely, the enormous stress on struggle, conflict, and high tension as positive values. Mao Tse-tung's commitment to these values probably preceded his conversion to Marxism-Leninism and has, as we know, even colored his vision of the utopian future which he seems reluctant to think of in terms of stasis and total

176

harmony. When directed against those defined as the outer enemy, struggle makes for solidarity "within the people." On another level, however, the enemy must be conceived of as ever present in the minds of the people itself in the form of "bourgeois thought." The struggle against this bourgeois thought is not only a negative factor. "Fighting against wrong ideas is like being vaccinated—a man develops greater immunity from disease after the vaccine takes effect, Plants raised in hot-houses are not likely to be robust." [3] At the time when it was uttered, this doctrine was linked to the lenient policies of the "Hundred Flowers" period. One can easily see how the same doctrine can be given a much more draconic interpretation.

Another element of the vision which is closely linked to the emphasis on spiritual transformation and collectivity is the stress on man rather than weapons or tools as the "decisive force in history." By transforming men's minds and consolidating their collective energies one can achieve enormous results in spheres where others have relied on material power. Here again the Yenan experience provides the shining example. Where one has mobilized the collective energies of men, motivated by the Maoist vision, economic advancement, national power, and social transformation are no longer purely dependent on "material prerequisites."

Another theme which has been stressed, with varying degrees of intensity, is the necessity of contact with the masses, and "participation in physical labor" on the part of intellectuals, students, professionals, and lower bureaucrats. This may reflect the genuine belief that "participation in labor" is a form of thought reform which will

[3] "On the Correct Handling of Contradictions among the People," *Communist China 1955–1959: Policy Documents with Analysis,* with a foreword by Robert R. Bowie and John K. Fairbank (Cambridge, Mass.: Harvard University Press, 1962), p. 289.

177

induce respect for physical labor and keep these elements from overweening pretensions. At the same time it is made crystal clear that one is not free to find among the masses any view of reality which contradicts the Maoist vision.

The Role of the Communist Party. Finally there is the enormous pivotal role of the Communist Party as the "proletarian" vanguard of society. Again, we seem to be dealing here with standard Marxist-Leninist doctrine, but, as has been pointed out by many, the party has probably played a more crucial and concrete role in China than in the Soviet Union at least during the lifetime of Stalin. The transformation of the Chinese people must be carried out by the party. Ideally speaking, the party maintains its supremacy not simply by dint of its organizational machinery but by its ability to internalize its "proletarian nature" into every party member. The "proletarian nature" of the party no longer resides, of course, primarily in the industrial workers but has become a kind of spiritual essence embodied in the party and yet still endowed with all those transcendental and universal qualities which Marx attributes to the working class. It is this idea of the "proletarian nature" of the party which sets strict limits to the whole populist drift of the Chinese vision. In fact since the beginning of the Sino-Soviet conflict, the party has stressed its proletarian nature more than ever. The party does not derive its transcendent moral status and historic role in China or in the world at large from the fact that it merely represents the Chinese people, but from a higher source. The party may serve the interests of Chinese nationalism but it does so from a supranational stance.

Within China itself the party ought to be the nervous system of society and should play a commanding role in every sphere of social and cultural endeavor. The ideal Communist cadre is not only a paragon of selflessness but potentially omnicompetent. Ideally it is also the party which is in direct communication with the "worker-peasant-soldier" masses and which reflects what the masses want and need or rather what they ought to want and need in a Maoist universe. Thus whenever there is a stress on the "mass line," one may assume that the decision-making function of the local party faction is being stressed. Yet all of this still leaves open the possibility that the party ranks, as opposed to the supreme leader, are vulnerable to error and backsliding.

Mao's Vision and Modernization. These it seems to me are some of the more salient elements of the Maoist vision. What have been the relations of this vision to the goal of modernization?

The official view of the present leadership is that the vision—no matter how its interpretation may fluctuate—not only provides the most effective means for achieving modernization, but is also an end in itself. The only desirable modernization is a modernization which can be incorporated into the Maoist vision. At the other extreme, we have the view that the vision runs completely athwart the prerequisites of modernization or that it is a sort of rationalization of the failures and difficulties of modernization in China. One makes a virtue of necessity according to this view because the necessity is intractable. Where weapons and capital are scarce, what is to be lost in stressing the organization of human energies? Where material incentives are not available, why not stress the "Communist ethic"? Oddly enough, the official ideology also seems to stress the relation of necessity to virtue. It was, after all, the peculiarities of Chinese conditions which made possible the stress on guerrilla warfare. It is the "poverty and blankness" of China, Mao insists in 1958, which makes possible the achievement of Communism long before the insidious corruptions of capitalism and revisionism have set in. The fact that "virtue" is associated with necessity by no means implies that the belief in virtue may not be genuine and fervent, particularly since the belief is also linked to the power interests of the leadership.

Surveying the history of the People's Republic since 1949, we find that various elements of the vision play an enormous role in the enormous effort of the first few years to bring about political and ideological consolidation. "Study," "thought reform," "confession," and so forth, were applied in various levels not only to prospective party members but to the "people" as a whole. The "small group" technique and the technique of mass organization were universally applied. The party seemed to be proving that totalitarian consolidation of a people could be carried out effectively by relying on "man" rather than technology. Except for those defined as counterrevolutionaries and reactionaries, there was considerable reason for belief that the spiritual transformation was succeeding. Some parts of the vision seemed, and seem, to be quite compatible with certain aspects of modernization. Many tasks of public health, police work, social control, and even economic undertakings, which depend primarily on labor intensity, lend themselves to Maoist methods.

The Relevance of the Soviet Model. However, while the vision did permeate large sectors of political and social activity, in the areas most crucial to the modernization effort—particularly as related to state power goals—it was the Soviet model which was followed. This involved some retreat in the concept of party omnicompetence, considerable emphasis on a "rational" division of labor and professionalization, and some emphasis on the need for a professional state bureaucracy. This does not mean that one should see an absolute antagonism between the Soviet model of modernization and the Maoist vision. Obviously the gravitation toward the total nationalization of industry and the collectivization of agriculture was entirely in line with both. In fact, it may well have been high confidence and exuberance (as well as a desperate sense of haste) induced by the success of his vision in the political and social spheres which led Mao and those closest to him in 1955 to feel that collectivization could be speedily consummated in China without the dire effects it had produced in the Soviet Union. The fact remains, however, that on the whole Mao modestly deferred to the "superior experience" of the Soviet Union in these areas.

With the beginning of the "Hundred Flowers" experiment, the picture becomes more complex. On the one hand the experiment seems to mark a further concession to the requirements of modernization. This can be discerned in the effort to give professionals and specialists a greater sense of security and freedom, in the rectification campaign directed against the party with the implied admission that in some areas the specialists knew more than the party, and even in the new concern with legal codification. The campaign also seems to have coincided, however, with some dawning doubts about the complete applicability of the Soviet model of modernization to Chinese conditions. These doubts were certainly encouraged by the death of Stalin and the new winds blowing in the Communist bloc itself. This new emphasis on the requirements of modernization as well as the doubts about the Soviet model did not, however, necessarily diminish the role of the Maoist vision. On the contrary, the "Hundred Flowers" formula was presented as a precious new contribution of Mao Tse-tung (the first since 1949) to the storehouse of Marxism-Leninism and it is, of course, quite easy to see how many ambivalent elements of the vision lent themselves to the "soft" interpretation of this period. In fact, Mao may have genuinely

181

believed that in the course of thought reform "the political outlook of the Chinese intellectuals has undergone a fundamental change." [4] The growing doubts about the complete applicability of the Soviet model of modernization may have even encouraged the view that the Maoist vision was applicable in areas where "Soviet experience" had hitherto reigned supreme.

In fact the "Great Leap Forward" and commune movement of 1957–1959 mark the high tide of the application of the Maoist vision to the very tasks of modernization. If the intelligentsia had shown its fundamental untrustworthiness, the subjective forces of the masses [5] were still available for heaven-storming feats. The emphasis on man as the decisive factor, on the negligible role of "material prerequisites," on the superior efficacy of collective subjective forces, and on the omnicompetence of the party all enter into this experiment, and give it its utopian, apocalyptic flavor.

Contraction and Revival. The retreat from the Great Leap in 1960–1962 again seems to mark a return to a sober estimate of the requirements of modernization but no longer on an exclusively Soviet model. It also seems to mark a contraction in the influence of the Maoist vision even though the new economic model with its emphasis on "agriculture as the base" was quite distinctly Chinese. One may, in fact, argue as has been suggested that the modernization policies of this period are much more "rational" in terms of Chinese realities than the policies of the Soviet period. They have led, it would appear, to a substantial

[4] Lu Ting-yi, "Let a Hundred Flowers Blossom; Let a Hundred Schools Contend," *Communist China 1955–1959*, p. 154.

[5] Whatever may have been the discontents revealed in 1956–1957, the peasants had, after all, been collectivized without producing anything resembling the effects of collectivization in the Soviet Union.

economic recovery. Yet, as we know, ever since the end of 1962 there has again been a rising crescendo of emphasis on "socialist education." At this very moment the Maoist vision, in one of its most extreme formulations, again occupies the center of the stage. The beginnings of this new revival are perhaps to be discerned in the crisis surrounding the army in the 1959–1962 period. As we know, P'eng Teh-huai, who seems to have become the spokesman of military professionalism and perhaps of professionalism in general, had also become an "antiparty" element, that is, a menace in the realm of power, while the crisis of morale in the army revealed in the *Bulletin of Activities* (*Kungs-tso T'ung-hsun*) documents suggested that the threat to the vision, at least in this sphere, was also regarded as a threat to power. Thus the campaign of "socialist education" was begun very early in the army, and having been judged a success, we find the army projected as a model for society as a whole. Here again we note what Stuart Schram has called Mao's "military deviation"—his tendency to think of a well-indoctrinated army as providing a paradigm of Communist life.

The return of large numbers of students to the country-side, involving as it did the frustration of hopes for advancement in urban society, also created a serious problem of morale which seemed to call for drastic therapy in terms of spiritual transformation. Beyond this, the growing intensity of the Sino-Soviet conflict has strongly impelled the leadership to project the Maoist vision onto the world at large as the very embodiment of "true Marxism-Leninism."

Above all, however, there is the fact that the aging Mao and those closest to him are genuinely concerned with the survival of the vision. The whole current fervid campaign of "socialist education" is permeated more by a kind of pervasive anxiety than by a mood of high confidence. The leadership may be quite optimistic about China's present economic situation and posture in the world at large, but it is precisely in the ideological sphere that one detects a mood of concern. The intelligentsia had shown its unreliability at the time of the "Hundred Flowers" campaign. Even the masses had shown their inability to live up to Mao's expectations at the time of the "Great Leap Forward." Indeed, it is now implied that the spontaneous inertial movement of things runs counter to the vision. "The restoration of capitalism," states Chou En-lai (and here he is undoubtedly the spokesman of Mao Tse-tung), "is not inevitable. In China we have a firm and fighting Marxist-Leninist Party, a proletarian Power which is increasingly consolidating itself, a powerful and revolutionary People's Liberation Army, an enormous number of cadres, a people of high political consciousness and a glorious revolutionary tradition. Of especial importance is the fact that our Party and State can count on a leading nucleus guided by the thought of Mao Tse-tung. All of this makes the restoration of capitalism very difficult in our country." [6]

There is here, of course, an oblique implication that the Soviet Union lacks these reassuring features. The whole thrust of the passage suggests, however, that what mainly stands between China and the "restoration of capitalism" is the Maoist vision. It is noteworthy that there is no reference to the "socialist structure" of Chinese society as one of the factors preventing such a restoration.

While the "socialist education" campaign has, however, fallen with an enormous weight on the literary, artistic, and cultural spheres and perhaps on all nonvocational areas of social life, while the cult of Mao has been raised to unprecedented heights, it is still not clear whether it has again been allowed to affect the strategy of modernization,

[6] "Report on the Work of the Government," *Peking Review*, Jan. 1, 1965.

particularly in the economic sphere. In fact, one may speculate that in the areas of highest priority—such as nuclear development—the Maoist vision has never been allowed to interfere with the requirements of technology. As far as one can judge at the present, experts are now expected to be diffused with redness even while devoting a maximum of attention to expertise, and the system of higher education is more oriented than ever to the production of experts. Yet all this may change. It would certainly be the gravest of errors to assume that because the 1960 economic strategy has proven fairly successful, economic considerations will necessarily override the concern with the "succession to the revolutionary heritage."

The leadership's concern is probably justified. It is difficult to believe that the vision will survive at least in its present extreme form. It is difficult to believe not only, or even primarily, because in some of its aspects it runs counter to the requirements of modernization. Even more immediately, it involves such a constricted and terribly simplified view of human life that one is inclined to doubt whether it is humanly viable. In terms of modernization, however, it is difficult to believe that the vision will be allowed in the long run to interfere particularly with those aspects of modernization most relevant to the achievement of national power. While the vision may retreat, however, we are in no position to foresee the extent of the retreat or to predict what will remain. Modernization may not be fully compatible with the Maoist vision but neither has it been fully compatible with Jeffersonian democracy. China may depart from the Maoist vision yet still move into a future uniquely its own. As long as Mao and those close to him remain at the helm, we may expect them to be as much concerned with the vision as with any of the other goals of the regime.

185

8

CHINESE VISIONS AND AMERICAN POLICIES (1966)

Washington is, of course, aware of Peking's hopes for the future; one is tempted to add, only too well aware. What might be called Mao Tse-tung's optimum global vision has only recently been called to our attention once more in Lin Piao's widely publicized article, "Long Live the Victory of People's Wars." [1] Here we find Asia, Africa, and Latin America enveloped by "wars of national liberation" strictly modeled on the classical pattern of the Chinese revolution. The ingredients of this classical model can be clearly enumerated. The war must first of all be led by a genuine Marxist-Leninist party (which now means a party oriented to Peking); the party must rely primarily on peasant support and establish rural base areas; the peasant-based people's armies must fight a type of guerrilla war which draws its basic inspiration from Mao's maxims on this subject; the people's war must also be supported by a

NOTE: This essay was first published in *Commentary*, April 1966.

[1] *Peking Review*, Sept. 3, 1965.

broad united front of "all those with whom one can unite" which will, however, remain firmly under Communist control. In this way the main enemy will be effectively isolated. In spite of Peking's continuing denunciations of Moscow's effort to "wave the baton" in the Communist world, one need not doubt that the Chinese themselves dream of waving the baton decisively in a world Communist movement reconstituted through the Maoist strategy and now centered on Peking.

In the face of assertions that Lin Piao's statement represents a newly proclaimed Chinese *Mein Kampf,* and in the interest of historical perspective, it is important to point out that all the essential features of this statement were contained in Liu Shao-ch'i's famous speech in 1949 to the meeting of the Asian and Australian wing of the WFTU. At the time, to be sure, the message was delivered within the limits imposed by a seemingly monolithic international Communist movement led by Moscow. Liu could, in fact, deliver the speech only because the Kremlin was for the moment itself lending a certain hesitant and suspicious support to the notion—rendered plausible by certain developments then current in Vietnam, Indonesia, India, and Malaya—of the applicability of the Chinese model to other areas of the non-Western world. It was made entirely clear, however, that the center of world Communist authority lay in Moscow. Since then, the inhibitions have been removed, and Peking has been able to proclaim its vision in all its imposing amplitude.

Nevertheless, that vision was probably more unambiguously plausible in 1949 than it has ever been since. The rapid retreat of the Western empire had just begun and by no means seemed inevitable (from the Communist perspective least of all). The isolated cases of Indian and Philippine independence could easily be dismissed by both Moscow and Peking as a bourgeois sham, and the hope that

187

rising nationalism would everywhere come under Communist leadership was vivid and reasonable. Ho Chi Minh was even then the paradigm of the popular nationalist leader who was also a convinced Marxist-Leninist.

The rise within the next few years of new states under non-Communist auspices and the failure of various Communist efforts in Asia subsequently led both Moscow and Peking to adjust their sights to a world which neither had foreseen. Out of this experience, there emerged the famous Bandung policy of cultivating Asian, African, and Latin American states already in being, whatever the nature of their internal polity. Bandung is often depicted as a triumph of Chou En-lai's suave diplomacy. If it was a triumph, however, it was a triumph of massive adjustment to an unlooked-for situation—hardly a triumph of the vision projected by Liu in 1949. Since Bandung, Peking's policies toward the third world have oscillated within the range of possibilities lying between the optimum vision and the Bandung line, while certain particular policies toward particular states can be explained quite satisfactorily in terms of the most conventional power politics. No doubt, the optimum vision remains the "esoteric" doctrine closest to Mao's heart. Yet there have been considerable stretches of time when the vision has been discreetly thrust into the background for the very solid reason that it is difficult to cultivate the existing states of Asia, Africa, and Latin America while simultaneously calling for their overthrow by "genuine" Marxist-Leninist wars of liberation.

In the Lin Piao statement the optimum vision does, to be sure, reemerge to the surface in full clarity—perhaps to encourage patience in Hanoi by stressing the "protracted" nature of the classical people's war; perhaps because at a time when the Bandung approach is generally not flourishing, a reaffirmation of the faith seems necessary; perhaps, again, because of the continuing need to distinguish Peking's "pure" line from the adulterations of Moscow. But whatever the real motive behind the restatement of the original vision at this time, a careful scrutiny of Lin Piao's article reveals the odd fact that, side by side with the maximum projection, ambiguities and ambivalences can be found which leave the doors wide open to alternative approaches. For example, having asserted that "national democratic" revolutions must be led by *genuine* "proletarian parties," having declared that *genuine* independence can be wrung from the imperialists only by "people's wars," and having contemptuously dismissed the socialist claims of all states not ruled by *genuine* Communist parties, Lin Piao avoids going on to draw any concrete conclusions. That is, he sedulously refrains from assigning the existing states of Africa, Asia (with the exception of India), and Latin America to the ranks of the "lackeys of imperialism"; nor is he likely to do so, as long as Peking continues to cherish hopes of a "Bandung" type conference in which it would play a leading role.

The Lin Piao document simultaneously gives expression to the optimum vision and to diluted versions of it. The original united front doctrine—the doctrine of "uniting with whom one can unite"—was meant to apply *within* given societies. In the diluted version, entire established nation-states are brought into the doctrine. Thus, the theme of the class struggle between rich and poor has been extended to "rich nations" and "poor nations." Very recently, even this conception was diluted by Mao's further extension of the doctrine to the not-so-poor nations of the "second intermediary zone" (Western Europe, Canada, and so on) which might conceivably be included in a vast united front against the main enemy—the United States.

While all this may appear to represent an enormously clever extrapolation of Mao's maxims, the fact remains that

189

uniting with "poor nations" is not the same thing as uniting with the poor. The genius of the Maoist united front strategy lay in its ability to combine absolute discipline and clarity of purpose in the core organization—the Chinese Communist Party—with a maximum of maneuverability vis-à-vis other social and polical groups *which it could effectively control.* The notion that the established states of Africa, Asia, and Latin America—no matter how poor—are as subject to direction from Peking as were the peasants of North China or the "Democratic League" during the late forties, is based on a false analogy between incomparable entities. On its immediate periphery China may, of course, exert the same types of coercive pressure which other great powers exert toward their weaker neighbors. This does nothing, however, to demonstrate the demonic effectiveness of the Maoist strategy. Indeed, in dealing with the whole "first intermediate zone," Peking has already discovered that a simple appeal to common poverty and to a colonial past will not automatically lead existing states with their own concrete conceptions of national interest, their own specific histories and preoccupations, and their own sensitive pride to accept Peking's "hegemony" in any international united front. Nor will it be at all easy to convince states which have had little experience with the United States in the past to think of it as Chinese patriots thought of Japan in the thirties and forties.

The ambiguities created by such dilutions pervade the Lin Piao document. Does the sensational assertion that North America and Europe now constitute—"in a sense"—"the cities of the world," while Asia, Latin America, and Africa constitute the "rural areas," refer only to the vast peasant masses of those latter regions, or does it also refer to the established regimes there? The answer is left in what is probably an intentional haze. No doubt, any regime willing to accept Peking's slogans will at least provisionally be included in the category of "rural areas" even if its polity be that of a feudal monarchy.

Even the concept of "war of national liberation" is subjected to dilution by Lin Piao. After stating flatly that people's wars must be led by the "proletariat," Lin Piao concedes, in passing, that "various classes [that is, non-Communist political elites] may lead people's wars against imperialism." Thus, in his list of countries which have undergone genuine "people's wars," Lin Piao is able to include Algeria and Indonesia (the Indonesia of the period before the recent coup), despite the fact that neither of these cases fits the classical model outlined elsewhere in the same article. In Algeria, it is true, the elements of armed revolution, guerrilla warfare, and base areas were present, but the most vital ingredient of all—the leading role of a "Marxist-Leninist party"—was missing, as it certainly was also in the case of Indonesia.

"War of national liberation" has become, then, one of those accordion-like terms which can be given either a strict or broad construction. Even states which have achieved independence by the most innocuous and pacific means may qualify as members of the anti-imperialist camp so long as they express the correct attitudes toward U.S. imperialism. A fortiori, Peking is likely to apply the term "war of national liberation" to almost any revolution or rebellion anywhere in the third world on the assumption that any violent disturbance can only propel the Chinese wave of the future and weaken the United States. It is one of the great triumphs of Peking's propaganda that Washington has come to agree with this view. If Washington had been in the same frame of mind with respect to "wars of national liberation" during the Algerian revolt, the United States would no doubt have thrown its full support behind the French policy of suppression.

191

In sum, then, the Lin Piao article simultaneously re-states Peking's maximum hopes and reflects all the adjustments which Peking has had to make to a world which —with the notable exception of Vietnam—has so far failed to shape itself to Chinese expectations.

But what of the future? The idea that the whole third world will easily succumb to China's infallible strategies has won ready acceptance among a large assortment of C.I.A. operatives, Pentagon strategists, professional Communist experts, games-theoreticians, political scientists, and others. Only yesterday, we had an enormous literature designed to show that the Soviet model and Soviet strategies would prove irresistible in the third world. It having since been discovered that Moscow must cope with a world as unpredictable and refractory to its own purposes as it is to ours, the same style of thought has now been transferred to China.

It would, of course, be utterly presumptuous to predict that the Chinese optimum strategy may not succeed in this place or that. The pressing question at the moment, however, is: which is the more dangerous—to predicate American policy on the fear that the whole third world is ripe for a "Chinese take-over" via the Maoist strategy, or to base it on the assumption that the third world is likely to develop in ways infinitely more varied and complex than anything dreamt of in Mao's philosophy? One would, at the very least, expect that arguments weighing against the Chinese projection would be given equal weight with arguments tending to support it. The great receptivity to the Chinese projection seems to rest, at least in part, on a theory which many of us share with the Chinese themselves—namely that the third world (whether it be described as "the rural areas" or the "underdeveloped" ones) is so homogeneous in its essential features that any political strategy which succeeds in one sector of this world may be expected to succeed in another. What is true of one underdeveloped, agrarian society is true of any other.

From some points of view, the features which all these societies have in common may indeed be of overriding importance. It is, however, extremely doubtful that the political destiny of any one of them can simply be deduced from the characteristics shared by all. The emergence and ultimate success of the Maoist strategy in China itself, for example, were made possible by certain very specific conditions existing in China during the thirties and forties —primary among them the failure of the Nationalist government to achieve firm military control within its own territory. This special feature of the Chinese political landscape, which helped to create and shape the Maoist strategy (as Mao himself has often admitted), is by no means universally present in the states of the "underdeveloped" world. Whatever may be their failures in other areas, many of these states (India for one) have proven quite capable of creating fairly unified and disciplined national armies. Apart from this, there is the fact that China, particularly North China, was subject during the forties to the Japanese invasion and that Japanese military power was subsequently dispersed in many directions; and there is the fact that Mao Tse-tung and his group not only developed their strategy, but were also superb implementers of it. The very combination of Marxism-Leninism and nationalism that characterized Mao and his group was itself a product of certain peculiarities of Chinese history during the twenties and thirties—peculiarities which there is no compelling reason to expect will be duplicated in the Nigeria of the sixties.

The Vietnamese case offers little real basis for generalizing, for the striking thing about Vietnam is that it has, to a unique degree, shared some of the characteristics of the Chinese situation. While the proximity to China must be given its own due weight in the history of Vietnam since 1945, the decisive point is the emergence of a shrewd, able, and ruthless Vietnamese Communist group which succeeded in gaining fairly effective control of a genuine Vietnamese nationalist movement. As indicated above, even in 1949, Ho Chi Minh's movement represented the only Communist operation in existence which closely approximated Liu Shao-ch'i's model. This movement continued to find support in certain segments of the population of the South who identified with it out of nationalist and other motives. Above all, it was able to apply its strategies against a regime which suffered from some of the same weaknesses as the Nationalist government in China. There was vast rural discontent, which Diem proved incapable of handling; there was his inability to unify and control his own military elite; and there were bitter communal divisions within the society which, while not resembling anything which had existed in China, produced effects similar to the regional fragmentation of power there.

But what of the other countries of Southeast Asia? They are all within geographical proximity of China, and none can afford to ignore the Chinese reality or the possibility of direct Chinese military intervention. To the extent, however, that Chinese hopes in this area still rely on the efficacy of the Maoist strategy, is it inevitable that Thailand—to take one case—must follow the path of Vietnam? In recent months there have been many reports suggesting that Peking is now "turning on" its strategy in Thailand. Behind all such reporting, of course, lies the assumption that the success or failure of the strategy depends on buttons pressed in Peking, even though we have little evidence to show that the spectacular rise of the Vietcong during the last few years has, in fact, had anything to do with immediate direction from Peking, however welcome it may have been to the Chinese. In assessing the potentialities of the strategy in

194

Thailand, therefore, it is the following questions which have to be examined. Does the Thai government effectively control its own armed forces and are these forces reasonably cohesive? Is there acute discontent in the countryside (outside of the much-discussed Northeast)? Is the direction of the incipient "people's war" in the hands of Thai leaders, or are Laotians, Vietnamese, and Chinese (in the South) playing a dominant role? These are the relevant questions, whatever the Chinese may wish and however the war in Vietnam may go.

It may, of course, be argued that even if the Chinese are not able to export Communism by exclusive reliance on their own revolutionary strategy, they will prove flexible enough to use other methods to achieve the same end. To do this, however, they will need more than those few precariously pro-Peking Communist groupings now in existence; a whole host of new Marxist-Leninist movements under effective Chinese control in places where they do not now exist will have to be created. The view that they will easily be able to create such a vast movement rests again on an unflagging belief in an ongoing entity called "world Communism" or "international Communism" which somehow has a life of its own over and above the sum total of actual Communist states and parties, and which remains unaffected by the vicissitudes of its constituent "detachments."

Involved in all this is a refusal to take the crisis which has erupted in the Communist world in recent years with real seriousness. Only yesterday, the phrase "world Communism" was generally used to describe an ostensibly monolithic power system centered on Moscow and based on the unquestioned authority of the Kremlin; the phrase referred not to a disembodied set of ideas, but to an organized movement. Now, however, one often encounters among those who speak of "world Communism" a view which conceives of

Communism as a kind of homogeneous unchanging substance which is, to be sure, subject to shattering but whose inner essence remains unchanged even after fragmentation. Since the substance remains the same the shattered parts may again be reassembled and resolidified at any moment (this time, presumably, under the leadership of Peking). Furthermore, the expansive capacity of the substance also remains unaffected by the experience of fragmentation. (It is no accident, incidentally, that many who argue most strongly for this particular view of "world Communism" were among those who most strongly insisted in the past that the system was monolithic and unbreakable.) However much they may come to differ, we are told, all Communist states share the aim of achieving Communism.

But what is Communism? Theoretically, the power to define what it is remains the exclusive prerogative of the Communist Party. In Communist ideology, the party is not merely a political organization: it is the embodiment of all those transcendental qualities which Marx attributed to the industrial proletariat. Whatever the good society may be, it can only be attained by the Communist Party, for it is the Communist Party which alone has access to the inner secrets of history and which can therefore apply infallibly correct solutions to the unfolding problems of history. As the embodiment of the general will of the proletariat, the party should be transnational and immune to inner conflicts of interest. These attributes of infallibility, universality, and unanimity have been the inner essence of the Communist Party as the ultimate mystery of Marxism-Leninism. Can one say that this mystery has remained unaffected by the recent crisis in the Communist world?

The Chinese, to be sure, have found a comforting precedent for the crisis in the history of Communism. Lenin, they say, often found himself in the minority within the Russian Social Democratic movement. He did not hesitate to break with the majority when the majority was wrong, and in the end his truth prevailed. Here again we find ourselves in the realm of false analogies. Can the relationship between vast Communist nation-states be compared with that between warring factions among Russia's Marxist intelligentsia? Will China be able to deal with the U.S.S.R. and its ideological claims in the manner in which Lenin disposed of the Mensheviks after October 1917? Will China be able, in any foreseeable future, to suppress the claims to Communist legitimacy of the Yugoslavs, the Poles, the Rumanians, or the Italian Communist party? The hard fact is that for all its pretensions (some quite spurious) to a purer Marxist-Leninist doctrine, Peking is doing quite as much as Moscow to undermine the transcendental status of the world Communist movement. The famous doctrine that the decisions of any given Communist party (that is, that of the U.S.S.R) are not universally binding on other Communist parties subverts not only Moscow's claims of central authority but *all* future claims of other potential centers of world Communism. It need hardly be pointed out that the slavish obedience to Moscow's line by foreign parties during Stalin's lifetime was not based on reasoned judgments that Stalin was always right, but precisely on the doctrine of the infallible authority of the Kremlin. Even if the Chinese do manage to create new pro-Peking Communist movements in Africa and Latin America, can they ever expect to exercise the type of authority over these groups which the Kremlin formerly exercised over the Communist world?

What is actually happening behind all the polemics is that the nation-state is asserting its primacy over the transnational claims of Marxism-Leninism while the very concept of an ultimate authority decays. To be sure, this still leaves open the possibility of the elaboration of national varieties of "Communism." The Maoist vision of the good society is one such variety; the day has passed, however, when one variety of national Communism is accepted without question as the mandatory image of the future even by "Marxist-Leninist" groupings.

The question of whether there can any longer exist an ultimate seat of authority in the "Communist world" and who—if anyone—will occupy this seat has now become the very heart of the Sino-Soviet conflict. It is probably not a question which can be resolved by compromises and agreements on the substantive issues which occupy the foreground of the polemics. But could it be resolved—as some have argued—by a reversal for the United States in Vietnam which would prove the Chinese contention that the U.S. is "a paper tiger" unable to cope with local "people's wars," disprove the Soviet position that American power must be respected even in this area, and convert the whole of "world Communism" to China's outlook? Even this is highly doubtful. For if it is meant that Moscow will itself be converted to Peking's outlook, it must be pointed out in the first place that Moscow's ideological position on "wars of national liberation" has by no means been as consistently "revisionist" as Peking would have us believe. Even now there is some question as to whether Moscow is, or is not, willing to lend support to Cuban-sponsored wars of national liberation in Latin America. In the improbable event that Moscow were to acknowledge Peking's correctness on this issue, Peking has guaranteed itself against the necessity of reconciliation by imposing on Moscow a whole catalogue of impossible conditions on other issues. As for the East-European Communist states and the Communist parties of Western Europe, which have adopted a generally "anti-Chinese" stance, they have done so for solid political reasons of their own, and they are not likely to be swayed into the "Chinese camp" by debaters' points. And finally, Peking's ability to create strong new Chinese-oriented Communist parties

throughout the third world will continue to depend on local conditions within that world and not merely on the
"demonstration" effect of Vietnam.

In sum, the Sino-Soviet conflict has—to use a term employed in the polemic—become a "hegemonistic" conflict.
The two principal actors have grown more concerned with
the question of who shall prevail than the question of who
is right. But this does not mean that either one or the other
must prevail, for both the Communist states and the Communist parties lying between the two are probably less and
less interested in having an ultimate source of infallible authority anywhere.

In emphasizing the enormity of the present crisis in the
Communist world, I have no intention of implying that the
world is "going our way," if by "our way" we mean the imminent universal enthronement of American-style liberal
democracy or European social democracy. The retreat of
empire has produced neither the Communist floodtide nor
the "Western" or "American" century. The major drift has
been in the direction of what might be called, for lack of a
better term, populist-nationalist dictatorships. Whether
their power rests on a single party or on the armed forces,
the leaders of such states invariably claim to incarnate the
will of the "people-nation." On many issues, no doubt, they
are closer to the Communist world than to ours. They generally profess adherence to "socialism," their anticolonial-
ism often draws on the Leninist vocabulary, and they often
find it expedient to denigrate the mere "machinery" of political democracy in favor of "organic" theories of representation.

One need not conclude, however, that this development
is in any sense "inevitable." Some societies may avoid it. All
one can say is that circumstances in many areas have been
favorable to it. Nor need one gratuitously idealize it as do

some elements of the "New Left," on the grounds that it is revolutionary and "socialist": some of these states may prove abominably corrupt, exploitative, and ineffective; others may be fairly effective in important areas and reasonably decent. Nor, again, need one be led by a dogmatic liberalism to assign them all to the Communist camp and refuse to coexist with them. The same development might well have occurred if Marx and Lenin had never lived, since the basic fund of ideas on which these leaders draw was, in fact, fully available in certain Left Jacobin-nationalist tendencies emerging out of the French Revolution. Ultimately, indeed, these ideas may turn out to be hardier than the more spectacular hybrid, Marxism-Leninism. Given the infinitely less intense and less transcendental nature of the ideologies governing the new states, there is a good chance that they may not go the whole way to totalitarianism, that they will prove more relativistic and technical-pragmatic in their economic approaches, and that they may also perhaps prove open in the long run to demands for personal freedom. Above all, one must remember that the overruling passion of these leaders is the passion to remain masters in their own households. This involves the refusal to accept any claims to hegemony—including spiritual claims—from outside. Since we, on our side, are presumably unburdened (or are we?) by an official philosophy which imposes on us the duty to universalize our own system, one would think that it would be a great deal easier for us than it would be for either Moscow or Peking to live with this passion for national autonomy.

It has, of course, been argued that all these regimes are simply halfway houses to Communism, and that the Chinese need but wait a little longer before an unstable third world —faced with enormous economic, demographic, and social problems—succumbs to Maoist strategies. No doubt, a minimum requirement for the survival of these states is that they show some movement in the direction of solving their problems, but it is far from certain that they must "solve" all of them immediately in order to remain viable. As a minimal *sine qua non*, they must demonstrate their power to maintain basic political and military control of the areas under their jurisdiction. But even where a given regime is overthrown, there is no reason to think that its successor will be less passionately concerned to maintain its own independence and autonomy. The notion that the Communist world possesses simple formulae for solving economic, demographic, and social problems which will prove irresistible in the third world is daily confounded by the growing diversity of "models" within the Communist world. The Chinese model (itself in a state of flux) no longer follows the Soviet model and does not resemble either the Yugoslav or even the Polish model. Fidel Castro, in spite of his adherence to Marxism-Leninism, has yet to find anywhere in the Communist world a ready-made model adequate to the concrete problems which confront him. Furthermore, while it continues to be represented as an ultimate and inevitable apocalypse or nemesis, the very nature of Communism has become highly problematic. Marxism-Leninism itself is proving a kind of halfway house to types of national "socialism" which oddly approximate some of the tendencies in the third world. There may arise in the future spiritual and social movements capable of bursting through the tough integuments of the nation-state framework, but one may strongly doubt whether the Communism we have known and experienced in the past can qualify any longer as such a movement.

I would suggest, then, that it is mistaken and dangerous to base American policy on the expectation that the whole third world is about to behave in a manner corresponding to Peking's optimum hopes for the future. It must be stressed again that these hopes are grounded not on the exportability of Chinese soldiers, but on the exportability of Chinese revolutionary strategy. Peking may staff its embassies with huge contingents of experts in "people's war" who will try to manipulate the "natives," but it has yet to be shown that the embassy staffs are quite that clever, or that the natives are quite that manipulable. Even in Southeast Asia where the Chinese can, and may yet, intervene with troops, Peking still fervently wishes to rely on the salability of its strategy. In Vietnam the strategy has, with adaptations, been quite effective—not because of buttons pressed in Peking or because of huge embassy staffs, but because of the very particular political history of Vietnam. Its effectiveness in other countries of Southeast Asia remains a function of internal situations in those countries, particularly if we assume the ongoing presence of American and Soviet power in the area.

Is Peking capable of adjusting to a world which does not correspond to its maximum hopes? Granted that in the mind of Mao and those closest to him the hopes are still active and real, the fact is that the process of adjustment has long since begun. The Bandung line of 1955 represented a major retreat from Liu Shao-ch'i's line of 1949. The current effort to cultivate commercial and even political relations with states of the Western world and with Japan can only be squeezed into Maoist categories by stretching these categories to the breaking point. Even the extraordinary concession which Peking has felt obliged to make to the principle of national independence and autonomy within the Communist world in the course of its polemics with Moscow constitutes an unacknowledged adjustment. In the eyes of Mao, these adjustments may represent temporary expedients which will soon be rendered unnecessary by the true wave of the future. There is, however, no need for us to accept Peking's assessment of their significance.

It nevertheless remains true that a minimum condition for Peking's adjustment to a world as recalcitrant to her most grandiose ambitions as it is to the ambitions of the rest of us is the recognition of China's status as one of the great world powers: a willingness—nay, an eagerness—to move as far as we can to involve and enmesh China, however harsh and unaccommodating its behavior may be, in whatever precarious structure of world order we have.

There is a reasonable possibility that, as a recognized great power, China would in the end come to accept its position in a world of nation-states large and small. To some, it may seem foolhardy to predicate foreign policy on "reasonable possibility" rather than on "policy science." I would simply urge that what we have on the other side is not science but unthinking extrapolation of the Chinese maximum vision, and a host of ill-considered clichés and stereotypes (put forth by people on various sides of the policy debate). We have, for example, the notion that whereas the Russians are "Western" (although they were considered "Oriental" by many only yesterday), the Chinese are occultly Oriental, or Asiatic. What conclusions one is expected to draw from this distinction, I do not know. A candid survey of the span of Chinese history leads to no firm conclusions on the question of whether the Chinese are more or less belligerent or more or less fanatical than Westerners: certainly, the imperial state was not more aggressive than the Czarist empire. We have the further stereotype that with its vast population, China must of necessity achieve world hegemony. From this, some have drawn the conclusion that we ought to recognize Chinese hegemony as quickly as possible, while others have called for the immediate dispatch of a few well-placed missiles. Then we have the notion that "Asia" must inevitably form part of a Chinese empire either because China controlled "Asia" in the past (which is false), or because Asians are all alike culturally or peculiarly prone to submit to those of superior strength. While China will undoubtedly play a leading role in Asian, and indeed world, politics, the fact is that Asia is not a political, and certainly not a cultural, entity: there are many states in Asia as little anxious to form part of a Chinese empire as states on other continents and probably as resourceful in avoiding this fate as others.

Finally, there is the more serious argument that the Chinese leaders still think of China as the center of civilization in a world of barbarians. Here I would point out that the cosmology of Chinese universal kingship on which this faith was founded has collapsed along with the world which made it plausible; that while Peking does regard itself as the center of an international faith, it is not the same faith which animated "sinocentrism" in the past (it is, in fact, a faith many of whose tenets are not even Chinese); and that the China of the present finds itself in a world which will continue to reject its "sinocentric" claims. These are all considerations, it seems to me, which may be quite sufficient to overcome the pull of mental habits inherited from the past.

I have not here attempted to put forth solutions to our Vietnamese dilemmas. Obviously, whether we regard Vietnam as the first "test case" in a chain reaction leading to a realization of the Chinese optimum vision, or whether we accept the reasonable possibilities suggested above, is a question which bears very strongly on the price—military, political, and moral—we are willing to pay to maintain our present position in that unhappy land.

9

UPHEAVAL IN CHINA (1967)

What lies behind the "Great Proletarian Cultural Revolution" of 1966? The news out of China seems nothing less than fantasic: vast hordes of the young and very young have suddenly been mobilized to carry out the spiritual transformation of Chinese society; a wholesale assault has been made upon the entire Chinese cultural heritage, as well as upon the "bourgeois" culture of the West, including everything from Bach to recent Soviet literature and modish hair styles. This movement has been attended by a hysterical, unrelieved scream of adulation for the person and thought of Mao Tse-tung as the single source of all wisdom, and by the revelation of a titanic political struggle involving some of the CCP's most prominent leaders and extending deep into the whole institutional apparatus of Chinese society. The official Chinese media have themselves emphasized with monotonous insistence the unprecedented revolutionary nature of what is happening. Every effort is being made to suggest that the People's Republic is turning a fresh page in its eventful history.

NOTE: This essay was first published in *Commentary*, February 1967.

205

Is all this nothing more than the surface reflection of an all-out conflict of power among individuals and groups eager to snatch the mantle of leadership from an enfeebled Mao? Is it a struggle between the army and the party? Does it represent an effort to achieve a maximum mobilization of the population in the face of what is felt to be the imminent possibility of war with the United States? Is it a response to a vast economic crisis hidden from our view? Or does the very phrase "Cultural Revolution" actually furnish some real clue to the nature of what is going on?

Before indulging in speculation as to the long-term implications of the "Cultural Revolution," we might remind ourselves that China has witnessed at least two such unpredicted shifts of course during the last decade. The "Hundred Flowers" campaign of 1956–1957 suggested a new policy of liberalization and relaxation; it was followed in 1957–1958 by the apocalyptic "Great Leap Forward" with its communes, backyard blast furnaces, and hints of total collectivization. Each of these departures was attended by unexpected consequences and sober reassessments. Together, they serve to warn us of the dangers that must accompany any attempt to assess the full impact of the "Cultural Revolution" on the vast masses of Chinese society, or its lasting effects.

We can, however, say something about the antecedents of the present "Cultural Revolution." For in spite of the emphasis on its novelty, many of its component themes may be traced to beginnings made in the period 1961–1962 and beyond that back to the issues raised by the "Great Leap Forward" of 1958.

In many ways, the "Great Leap Forward" represented Mao Tse-tung's finest hour. This is not to discount the overwhelming victory of 1949, the successful application of Maoist methods to the vast tasks of political consolidation and organization, or the seemingly successful Maoist effort to "remold" the mental outlook of an entire population. Yet, as the government turned its attention in the early fifties to the tasks of modernization, there was always discernible a modest deference to "superior Soviet experience." Shortly after the takeover, Mao remarked soberly: "Things in which we were well versed will soon be needed no longer and we shall have to do things in which we are not well versed." In all these matters the Soviet Union played the role of teacher, not only because this was a condition of the alliance with Stalin, but also, no doubt, because of a genuine Chinese belief in Soviet experience. Thus, while the last decade of Chinese Communist history has been marked by erratic departures and sweeping experiments, the first seven years seemed to move steadily toward an ever-increasing Sovietization of Chinese life.

After 1955, however, it would appear that serious questions arose (in the more lenient atmosphere made possible, no doubt in part, by the death of Stalin) concerning the total applicability of Soviet methods to Chinese problems, particularly to Chinese economic problems. The new feeling was that Chinese methods had to be found for dealing with Chinese difficulties. By the end of 1957—after the demise of the "Hundred Flowers" experiment—we find the gradual emergence of new approaches in the economic sphere, particularly in the area of rural economy. These approaches, which were ultimately to culminate in the spectacular commune experiment of 1958, were designed to cope with the very real and intractable problems of Chinese agriculture and China's huge population; they seemed, moreover, to involve the application of Maoist maxims and teachings to areas where Soviet wisdom had hitherto prevailed. Just as the Red Army had won its victories by depending on men rather than weapons, the peasants were now expected to win their war against the land by mobilizing vast human energies rather than by relying on material

207

resources. Like the guerrillas of the past, who sacrificed their petty interests to the larger cause with little thought of remuneration, the peasant masses, in their devotion to the new state, could be induced to put forth their maximum energies without the promise of material incentives. Filled with ardor and enthusiasm, the peasant would exercise all his initiative and ingenuity to fulfill his production tasks. In this effort he would be directly led and inspired, as in the old Yenan days, by party cadres thoroughly imbued with a selfless Communist ethic, and capable of exercising leadership in the most diverse areas of economic, social, and cultural activity.

It now seemed possible that the same Maoist maxims which had worked so well in the idyllic days of Yenan (at least, as viewed through the lenses of Mao's nostalgic idealization) and in the postwar period of consolidation would be equally effective in pushing forward China's economic development. This possibility in turn opened up utopian perspectives, so that it can be said that in 1958 Mao experienced what might be called his full beatific vision. The vast hinterlands of China would be organized into a gigantic network of communes, each one a self-sustaining economic, cultural, and even military cell. These cells would be held together and led forward by the monolithic hierarchy of the Communist Party, whose members embodied both the highest Communist virtues and the greatest technical versatility. The collective solidarity of the masses would be further welded by a sense of militant solidarity against the enemy without.

Needless to say, this image of the society as an armed camp of comrades-in-arms, united in clear-cut conflict against the ubiquitous reactionary enemy, was an integral part of the total vision. Within such a society, the role of the professionals and of the academic and literary intelligentsia—a stratum which had demonstrated its essential unreliability during the "Hundred Flowers" campaign—would be reduced to a minimum. Professionals and academic experts were not only guilty of presuming to lay claim to autonomous areas of knowledge (which they used to place themselves outside of and above the party), but were also inclined to selfish careerism and personal vanity. Built into their outlook—according to the new "vision"—was an exaggerated emphasis on "objective" difficulties and a kind of antiseptic neutralism directly antagonistic to the official view of China and the world—a view which stressed the titanic struggle between the forces of good and the forces of evil. The individualistic vanity of intellectuals and literary men had led them to a constant pursuit of irony, ambiguity, and complexity—qualities which are the enemies of simplicity—and into a concern for their petty personal destinies. They represented much of what was most obnoxious in modern Western urban civilization. China must achieve wealth, national power, and Communism while at the same time restricting and by-passing such baleful influences.

It might be added in passing that Mao himself has always been somewhat more complex than his vision. He has not been immune to all the joys of the flesh or the vanities of individual glory. A literary man of no small vanity, he has allowed himself to write traditional symbolic poetry in a style not permitted to others, and in his encounters with foreigners has often suggested that his apprehension of reality is somewhat more ironic than the grand simplicity of his vision would appear to indicate.

One important aspect of the "Great Leap Forward" was its innovations in the sphere of foreign policy. The period was marked by a new and basic consistency of spirit (a consistency which had not always existed) between internal and external policy. Just as China was now expected to overcome all internal obstacles by a massive mobilization of "subjective" forces, so too on the global scene the Communist bloc was expected to join forces in a policy of bold confrontation with imperialism. This posture was, of course, still based on a fundamental belief in the solidarity of the bloc and on the assumption of long-term cooperation between the Soviet Union and China.

As we know, the utopian hopes of the "Great Leap" were never realized, but rather gave way to the massive retreat and the severe economic crisis of the 1959–1962 period. Given the soaring hopes of 1958, one cannot but feel that the retreat must have occasioned the profoundest chagrin on the part of Mao Tse-tung. Those who came under attack in 1959 were precisely the "Right opportunists" (the most prominent of them was P'eng Teh-huai) who had been least enthusiastic about the "Great Leap" and who were evidently now saying, "I told you so." Even now it would appear that the "Right opportunists" of 1959 remain one of the main targets of the proletarian "Cultural Revolution."

By 1960, the retreat was well underway. In the economic sphere it involved a decentralization of the communes and a striking new emphasis on the primacy of agriculture over industry and on material incentives for peasants in the form of private plots and free markets. It was a sober and realistic response and quite originally Chinese. It certainly did not involve a return to the Soviet model. As with all such major shifts in the past, it also seemed to involve reversals of policy in other areas of social and cultural life. Students were now told to devote themselves to their studies, and to respect elderly professors. The stock of "expertise" rose, particularly in the economic and scientific spheres. Academic historians were again encouraged to treat the problems of Chinese history with a certain limited degree of freedom. We can only speculate on Mao Tse-tung's relationship to all this. In spite of his utopian visions, he has always in the past been able to recognize intractable facts when they stare him in the face. One may surmise that in the economic sphere he acquiesced to the new policies while perhaps holding his silence in that other vast sphere which the Chinese now call "cultural."

It is important to note that even at the height of the period of retreat there were certain obvious areas of dissonance. It was, of course, precisely during the 1960–1962 period that the Sino-Soviet crisis came to the surface. Peking was rapidly moving from a rejection of Soviet policies to an assertion of its own authority as the bearer of true Marxism-Leninism. Even now, one of the peculiarities of the relationship between the Soviet Union and China lies in the fact that they still remain enmeshed with each other through their conflicting claims to possessing the one truth. This means that internal domestic policies cannot be divorced from "foreign relations." One need not doubt the sincerity of the Chinese leadership when it began to see a relationship between the errors of Soviet world policy and domestic Soviet "revisionism"; and when the Soviets, for their part, attacked the "Great Leap Forward" and its utopian mystique, it was not only because they regarded it as economically unsound but also because they could not afford to ignore what they considered to be Mao Tse-tung's "petty bourgeois," distorted image of the good Communist society (just as the Chinese could not later ignore Khrushchev's "bourgeois" vision of Communism). The Soviet Union, in Mao's view, was sliding back into capitalism because it had placed all its reliance on institutional conditioning and had neglected the spiritual transformation of the masses. If China had its own message for the world, it was one which called for more, rather than less, emphasis on the ideological—or, as it is now called, the "cultural"—factor; it was, in effect, the message of the "Great Leap Forward."

We now know that the universalization of Mao's teachings in 1958 also embraced the military sphere. Here too, the Soviet model—with its emphasis on professionalism, technical proficiency, and basic control by the officer corps—was to give way to party dominance ("politics in command"), an emphasis on the spiritual training of the soldier, a downgrading of the officer corps, and participation by the army in all sorts of social activities. This reversion to the maxims of Yenan was, to be sure, balanced by the determination to achieve a nuclear capacity, and in 1958 still presupposed cooperation with the Soviet Union in the event of war. In this sphere, however, despite the general failure of the "Great Leap Forward," there was to be no retreat. As late as August 1959, P'eng Teh-huai, Minister of Defense and defender of military professionalism (and professionalism in general), was overwhelmingly defeated. Neither the deterioration of relations with the Soviet Union, the termination of Soviet nuclear aid, nor the serious crisis of morale in the army during the 1960–1961 period, was to lead to any departure from the Maoist line in the army. On the contrary, the failure of morale in the face of adversity was laid to the woeful neglect of the spiritual training of the average soldier; a new emphasis was required to place "politics in command."

The Maoist line in military affairs has implications both for military strategy and for internal policy. Unless one assumes that the Chinese expect to put their modest nuclear arsenal to use in the near future, one must suppose that their present nuclear development is an aspect more of political than of military strategy. It represents a defiance of the American-Soviet nuclear monopoly, and a demonstration of what China can do in the sphere of advanced technology. The Yenan concept of mass military organization also seems to involve a fundamentally defensive posture vis-à-vis a possible American attack. In the event of war, the Americans are to be drawn into the endless expanses of

China and worn down in the course of a protracted people's war. This strategy does not preclude the use of Chinese arms abroad in situations where Chinese superiority is clear and great-power intervention unlikely—as in the case of the Chinese invasion of India. Nor does it imply that China may not intervene in Vietnam in the event of further escalation. It does, however, imply an effort to avoid rather than to seek a confrontation with American power.

Yet it must be stressed that the main significance of the Maoist military line may have lain in its application to internal affairs. Mao was determined not to retreat in the crucial military sector, and it was as the implementer of Mao's line in the army during the most critical period of 1959–1961 that Lin Piao was to lay the basis for his present ascendancy. Army loyalty is, of course, crucial in any state, but behind Mao's concern with the military lay an even deeper conviction harking back, once again, to the Yenan days. The Yenan experience had shown that a well-indoctrinated People's Army provided an ideal school for inculcating Communist virtues. If the spirit built into the guerrilla enterprise—a spirit of self-sacrifice, collectivity, simplicity, fortitude, and initiative—could be fostered and brought to high consciousness by zealous party cadres, then the average soldier and the average military unit could also become models of individual and collective behavior for the society as a whole. This vehement emphasis on spiritual training in the army might itself indicate that Mao had not really accepted the retreat of 1960 even in the cultural sphere and was already envisaging the possibility of turning the army into a model of Maoist conduct for the whole of Chinese society.

In fact, the entire period between 1961 and the present has been marked by a slow but steady accretion of all those themes and motifs which have now culminated in the "Cultural Revolution." I am not suggesting here that there was a prearranged, unfolding plan. At least in part, the growing vehemence and shrillness of this "cultural" effort may be directly due to the massive resistance which similar efforts have met from every quarter of society since the retreat from the "Great Leap Forward." As early as 1961, however, attempts were made to diagnose the failure of the "Great Leap Forward" in a manner which, though acknowledging the role of natural disasters and local mismanagement, still placed major blame on the failure to have imbued the masses with a true Communist ethic. Mao himself, it seems, had overestimated the spiritual preparedness of his people. What was required now was a longer, more sustained effort to internalize Mao's "proletarian" conception of man in the very souls of the masses. This effort began, as we have seen, in the military sector, but it was not until the Plenum of the Central Committee in September 1962 that the counterattack against "cultural" relaxation became plainly visible. (It may have been facilitated by the modest recovery brought about by the sober economic policies of the post-1960 period.) By 1963, we already have the slogan, "Learn from the People's Liberation Army." The work of Lin Piao's General Political Department in the army had been pronounced a success, and the army was now ready to play its role in the society at large. Men who had undergone a supposedly successful moral transformation while serving in the army were to be brought into every area of social life. The cultural department of the PLA was to play an increasingly important role in the arts.

The years 1963–1964 also saw the emergence of two soldierly models of Communist virtue, Lei Feng and Wang Chieh, together with their conveniently available diaries. A perusal of these diaries and of the three "works" of Mao which are now stressed above all others (the "three much-read works" —"In Memory of Norman Bethune," "On Serving the People," and "On the Foolish Old Man who Removed the Mountains")—indicates that since 1962 the military, economic, and political doctrines of Mao Tse-tung have become less important than his sermons on the Communist moral transformation of the individual. Despite the inability of many Westerners—themselves profoundly habituated to thinking of human affairs in terms of institutional devices and social conditioning—to credit Mao's belief in the effectiveness of these moral sermons, it nevertheless appears that he has indeed committed himself to this program in a genuine and wholehearted manner.

Also in 1963, growing prominence began to be attributed to the campaign for "socialist education" in the countryside. Concern over the "spontaneous tendency to capitalism" inherent in the institution of private plots and free markets had probably been present for some time; indeed, there is evidence that in Mao's own province of Hunan, the effort to counteract this tendency had begun as early as 1960, and involved mobilizing those designated as "poor and lower-middle" peasants to attack all excessive commitments to private activities. It would appear that, in an adumbration of the later role of the "Red Guards," youngsters and schoolchildren were also employed in the work of ideological pressure. Although it is impossible to ascertain the precise nature and limits of this campaign, the institution of private plots—one which has played a crucial role in the Chinese economy—has still, so far as we know, not been abolished, despite the sustained effort at moral condemnation.

The "counterattack" in the more strictly intellectual sphere was also well under way by 1963, as historians and philosophers began to be excoriated for manifold bourgeois errors. Needless to say, a dominant theme in this whole Maoist cultural effort was that of Soviet decadence. The Soviet Union had by "negative example" proved the remark-

215

able thesis that an "advanced social system alone cannot accomplish much without a revolutionary change in man himself." [1] In short, one can say that all the assumptions and essential themes underlying the present "Cultural Revolution" were on the scene by the beginning of 1965.

Yet, as we also know, the economic policies inaugurated after 1959 remain essentially intact even now. Has this hesitation to interfere with prevailing economic policies been due solely to a powerful resistance to change within the hierarchies of the party or the government? Or has Mao himself, after the failures of 1958, hesitated to launch new experiments in the economic area? While the assertion that the "revolutionization of the masses" will release enormous productive energies has been repeated again and again during the last few years, Mao himself may have accepted the fact that China's general economic development will actually be slow, and may hence have decided to concentrate upon laying the spiritual foundations of a Maoist society while leaving the economy alone. Technical experts were exhorted to base all their efforts on the "Thought" of Mao Tse-tung but to keep their minds steadily fixed on the actual task at hand. At any rate, the question of the relationship between "class struggle" in the cultural sphere and in economic practice is still unresolved.

In sum, then, I would suggest that the stage had already been set for recent developments by the beginning of 1965. Yet clearly there have been new developments since then. Are these new developments simply a spectacular culmination of the evolution described above, or have more recent events—particularly American large-scale intervention in Vietnam—played a crucial role? While the possibility of a war with the United States has never been overlooked, the

[1] Lao Chu, "The People's Communes Making Progress," *Hung Ch'i*, Feb. 1964.

actual prospect of imminent conflict became real only with the arrival of large numbers of American troops in Vietnam. It was quite conceivably this new prospect which reactivated the hidden debate on military strategy. In spite of constant assertions about the total success of the Maoist line in military policy, professional military opposition was far from dead. Indeed, the statement made by Chief of Staff Lo Jui-ch'ing in May 1965, entitled "Commemorate the Victory over German Fascism!" seems in retrospect of considerable significance.[2]

This article praised the performance of the Soviet Red Army (hardly an army run on Maoist lines) during World War II and laid particular stress on its capacity "to destroy the enemy at his starting point, to destroy him in his nest." The article therefore also appeared to suggest that China itself requires a military apparatus capable of taking the offensive against an American enemy rather than simply waiting to wear him down in the heartland of China. It might also have suggested the possibility that China is willing to entertain the notion of limited cooperation with the Soviet Union in modernizing China's army and in taking a united stand against the U.S. in Vietnam. (It should be added, however, that this particular variety of professionalism and possible "pro-Sovietism" need have no "moderate" implications whatsoever for future Chinese-American relations.)

In any event, if such a debate on military strategy did indeed occur in the Chinese government, and if it involved wide circles of the governing elite, it would certainly have called to Mao's attention the degree to which there continues to be resistance—at least in one sector—to his program of spiritual transformation. It is clear, however, that Vietnam did not change Mao's own perspectives by one

2 Published in *Peking Review*, no. 20.

iota. Therefore, while the possibility of war with the United States may have intensified and exacerbated certain previously existing debates, and revealed the extent of the opposition to the "Thought of Mao Tse-tung," it did not change the terms of the debate itself. At most, it may have driven Mao further into that sense of exasperation which culminated in the "Cultural Revolution" of 1966.

It is also possible that resistance to Mao in 1965 may have manifested itself in fields other than that of military policy. The fact that the third five-year plan was to be launched in 1966 must have turned attention to economic matters. Mao's insistence on "culture" may not have seriously affected ongoing economic practices, but it certainly involved an enormous diversion of emotional and mental energies from economic concerns. In the sphere of education, for instance—an area vital to the economy—the increased emphasis on labor and on spiritual training represented a diversion of energies from the vocational training of experts. It is interesting to note that while the start of the five-year plan was announced in January 1966, the amount of attention devoted to economics in the public media since then has been minimal. It is quite likely that strong resistance was felt in this sphere as well, and that a man like P'eng Chen, who was happy to endorse the "revolutionization" of the Peking Opera, was less than enthusiastic about the even greater insistence on "Mao's Thought" in the spheres of economics and education.

From Mao's point of view, the most crucial area of all was the cultural one; here, too, there had been considerable evidence of resistance and foot-dragging on the part of all those party organs (aside from the army) concerned with cultural affairs. "Mao's Thought," to be sure, dominated the foreground, but the cultural "monsters and demons" who had revealed themselves during the 1960–1962 period of relaxation were still on the scene. Now, as in the past, Mao has tended to seek primary symptomatic evidence of the health of Chinese society as a whole in the area of its culture—particularly in literature. Thus, the continued resistance of "bourgeois" tendencies in Chinese life to Mao's vision seems simply to have made the leader more grimly determined than ever to push through his own ideas. Lin Piao's famous tract of September 1965, "Long Live the Victory of People's War," and the all-out attack on the writer, Wu Han, which began in November 1965, may both be considered as aspects of this more vehement counterattack. Lin Piao's article is, of course, mainly an exposition of the Maoist analysis of world developments, but it must also be seen as a response to domestic critics. It consists of a grandiose application of the Yenan model to the world at large and projects a world situation favorable to the triumph of this model. Although uncompromising in spirit, it does not anticipate the export of Chinese armies to foster Maoist revolutions abroad. Rather, it assumes a third-world situation favorable to the spread of the Maoist model of revolution, or—on a more immediate level—the acceptance of Chinese leadership by established governments in many of the world's "poor countries." It emphasizes the importance of Vietnam as a test case of Maoist revolution but also stresses the need for Vietnamese self-reliance. Finally, it emphatically confirms the need to continue along Maoist military lines at home.

The attack on Wu Han was to be the direct antecedent of the "Cultural Revolution." Historian, vice-mayor of Peking, and part-time *littérateur*, he had written a play in the dark days of 1960 (published in 1961) with a historical setting in the Ming dynasty; the play has since been interpreted (probably correctly) as an assault on the "Great Leap Forward" experiment. In November of 1965, a decision was taken to make of Wu Han and his play a "negative example" of all that was wrong in the cultural sphere. Wu Han himself, however, had been closely connected to cultural figures in the Peking Party Committee machine headed by P'eng Chen; the attack may therefore have been merely a surface manifestation of the larger power struggle already taking place behind the scene. Or, if we credit the official account, it may have been launched in all sincerity, and then aggravated by the fact that the leadership of the Peking Party Committee failed to join in with the proper enthusiasm, thereby revealing its own bourgeois proclivities. There have, after all, been previous instances of the use of literary figures as "negative examples" (for example, Hu Feng, Yü P'ing-po), without any evidence of titanic power struggles in the background.

In any case, whether it was the Wu Han affair which brought the leadership struggle to a head or whether the affair was a manifestation of a struggle already under way, it is clear that by spring 1966 the power struggle was already visible. The nature of that struggle, however, was not yet apparent. Was it a horizontal struggle among different individuals and groups—and has Mao therefore been merely an instrument of the struggle itself? Was it a sheer power struggle, unrelated to issues? Or could it be described as a struggle between institutional entities such as the army and the party? The notion of a horizontal struggle for succession is based on the assumption that Mao himself has not played a decisive role in current events, or that he is a figurehead. My entire argument, on the other hand, has been grounded on the premise that now, as in the past, Mao has played a decisive role. Although he may at times withdraw himself expediently from the forefront of affairs, as he did in the early sixties, when he decides to bring his power to bear on any matter he does so with crushing weight. A most recent sensational revelation from a Japanese source cites a statement, presumably from Mao himself, that his authority within the party had been usurped by Liu Shao-ch'i, Teng Hsiao-p'ing, and others ever since the famous Wuhan meeting of December 1958, at which time he resigned his position as chairman of the CCP. Because of the convulsive conflict now raging in Peking, we must treat Mao's own accounts with as much skepticism as those of all other participants. There seems to be little doubt that Mao played a dominant role in the attack on P'eng Te-huai and the "Right opportunists" in 1959, and there is every reason to believe that he brought his full authority to bear on military policy during the 1960–1962 period. Mao's style of thinking is stamped upon the whole Sino-Soviet conflict. It may well be, however, that the end of the "Great Leap Forward" was indeed marked by a more vociferous opposition in high councils to Mao's policies than had hitherto been the case, and that Mao has found it judicious on occasion to bow to his opposition on certain matters, particularly at moments of uncertainty on his own part. The charge that Liu, Teng, and others wholly usurped his infallible authority now constitutes another, particularly heinous, item in the list of charges being drawn up against them.

I would suggest therefore that Lin Piao occupies his present position because he has been promoted by Mao on the basis of his proved abilities as the implementer of the Maoist line in the army—not because he had recourse to a well-oiled political machine. Nor can Lin Piao's rise be considered part of the ascendancy of the "army" as such. He has made his fortune as the representative of the Maoist line, not as a representative of the "army" itself (that is, the officer corps), which, one gathers, is as internally divided as other institutional segments of society. Nor does Lin Piao represent the party. Indeed, the extent to which the whole "Red Guard" movement is being used as a power weapon by Mao and Lin against the established institutions of society argues for the view that Lin did not have a preestablished power base of his own. I would further suggest that

221

T'ao Chu, the chairman of the South Central Bureau of the party, has also risen because of his proved merits as a servant of Mao's cultural policies, particularly in the sphere of "socialist education" in the countryside. As of now, however, we have the additional news that T'ao Chu himself is currently out of favor; here, one can only offer the suggestion that, with the mounting frenzy of the conflict, even those who have proved themselves worthy in the past may yet come to seem unreliable if they oppose certain of the more extreme developments of their leader's "Cultural Revolution." It is possible that T'ao Chu has placed himself in opposition to efforts at bringing the "Cultural Revolution" to bear within the economic realm itself. We are dealing with a situation in which it is quite possible to go astray by standing still.

As for those now in the opposition, all of them have been, at one time or another, faithful mouthpieces of Maoist policies. Cultural Commissar Chou Yang, for example, the scourge of China's writers since the early forties, was always considered the spokesman of Mao's most Stalinist ideas in the realm of literature. P'eng Chen, until recently, was a leading spokesman on both domestic and foreign policy. Lo Jui-ch'ing, former chief of the secret police, had helped Lin Piao implement the Maoist line in the army during the early sixties. Needless to say, the past public statements of these men had always been designed to conform as closely as possible to the Communist convention of total unanimity.

It is true, however, that P'eng Chen, Lo Jui-ch'ing, and Chou Yang had become closely associated with certain particular constellations of interests—P'eng Chen with the Peking Party Committee (which plays an extraordinarily important role in culture and higher education), Lo Jui-ch'ing with the officer corps, and Chou Yang with the culture and propaganda apparatus. The danger here did not lie simply in the creation of what Mao calls "independent kingdoms." Certainly, P'eng Chen's ample powers were not wholly dependent on the Peking Committee. But the day-to-day association with "authorities" involved in professional tasks may have dampened whatever ardor these men originally had for the ever more vehement emphasis on the "Thought of Mao Tse-tung," and may have resulted in giving them a new sense of solidarity with their professional protégés. Whether or not P'eng Chen truly sympathized with the writings of Wu Han, Teng T'o, and others, he might well have questioned the need for a whole campaign against them. Here questions of policy become hopelessly intertwined with questions of power.

It is, to be sure, somewhat difficult to think of Chou Yang as a defender of the professional writer or artist, yet these "cultural workers" have, in fact, constituted his "kingdom." He may be a literary Stalinist, but Mao's ideas on art and literature have gone well beyond the frontier of Stalinism. In spite of all his repressive measures, Stalin accepted the conventional "bourgeois" conception of the author and artist; Mao, of course, envisions a literature of "workers, peasants, and soldiers" written for immediate purposes. In practice, this means a kind of literature turned out by committees of trained propagandists. We know that in the last few years many theatrical and literary activities have been taken in hand by the Cultural Department of the General Political Department of the PLA, thus by-passing the jurisdiction of the conventional party cultural organs. It would seem plausible under these circumstances that even Chou Yang may have demonstrated something less than singlehearted dedication to Mao's "Cultural Revolution." It is, in fact, interesting to note that the main visible targets of the "Cultural Revolution" on the lower regional and provincial levels of party organization have been party functionaires, concerned with cultural and propaganda affairs. Foot-dragging, one would gather, has been a characteristic of the whole party cultural apparatus from top to bottom. This would also indicate that the issue of "culture," as Mao understands it, is at the heart of the present convulsion.

Something must be said about the political survival of the durable Chou En-lai. Chou, it seems to me, continues to be an indispensable resource man. The Mao-Lin projection of the world's future may be based on profound faith in the verdict of history, but in the short run one must deal with the world situation as it is. One negotiates with Pakistan and seeks trade with Japan and attempts to exercise as much influence as possible under prevailing circumstances. Chou En-lai has always performed a crucial role in this area. His continued presence may also indicate that the forces which are determined to keep the "Cultural Revolution" and the "Red Guards" within some bounds are still vastly powerful and resistant.

What is suggested, therefore, is that there has probably not been an aggressive effort on the part of an opposition to seize power, but that ever since the early sixties there have been various forms and degrees of resistance to Mao's determined effort at placing his vision of man and society in the forefront of attention; that this resistance has manifested itself in all institutional sectors of Chinese society, including the party; and that this ongoing resistance (which may even have increased in 1965) has confirmed the aging Mao in his profound suspicion of the inertial "bourgeois" tendencies latent in all existing institutions and in all those involved with institutional responsibilities. One need not doubt that men like Teng Hsiao-p'ing, Liu Shao-ch'i, and P'eng Chen—men who had reason to cherish the highest private ambitions—must have deeply resented Lin Piao's ascendancy, but it seems to me quite impossible to separate the struggle for power from the issues involved.

The events leading up to the emergence of the "Red Guards" seem to have followed the major high-level purges. A new effort was now exerted to transform the soul of China and arm it against the forces of inertia. In June 1966, the West became aware of struggles within Peking University and other institutions of higher learning against "revisionist" academic administrators and students, struggles in which it was, of course, the young people who were mainly involved. It is evidently out of such struggles that the "Red Guards" emerged. Youth was to be rescued from the clutches of the revisionists—including those in control of the Communist Youth League—and made the bearer of the "Cultural Revolution." Only youth—particularly the very young—remained fresh and untainted. In spite of the continuing rhetoric about the masses, it would appear that the older and middle generations of these masses had proved themselves as susceptible as the institutional elites themselves to the corrupting pull of mankind's past.

If youth was to help revolutionize society, however, it had to undergo the actual experience of revolution. Here we note a theme which had emerged as early as 1964, when, in response to American assertions about the more reasonable, pragmatic nature of the coming generation in China, and to the ominous example of Soviet youth, a new set of slogans appeared: "Everything must be done to make the youth succeed to the revolutionary heritage of the past." "One can learn to swim only by swimming [a slogan which reminds us of Mao's symbolic swim in the Yangtze]; one can learn to be revolutionary only by making revolution." One might say that the ethos of revolution is itself the ethos of Communism. Thus, the activities of the "Red Guards" represent, among other things, an effort to create within a vastly different environment a substitute for the revolutionary experiences of Mao's generation. This whole

225

movement is soaked in nostalgic allusions to the difficult yet golden days of the thirties and forties. Such phrases as "little generals" and "Red Guards" themselves refer back to the charming waifs who were attached to the Red Army during the old guerrilla days and who served that army with selfless devotion.

The "Red Guard" movement thus serves many purposes. It is used as a lever of power by Mao and Lin Piao against the resistant elements which permeate all the institutions of society. The enthusiasm and intolerance of the young are to be used to convey to the society at large the purest and most exclusivist image of Mao's vision of man and society. Finally, the "Red Guard" movement provides the young with an unforgettable revolutionary experience. One should not make too much of the notion that the "Red Guards" are the auxiliaries of Lin's thoroughly transformed People's Liberation Army. In fact, the army leadership continues to be as suspect a sector of the elite as any other, and there have been many reports of local army resistance to the "Red Guards." For the moment, the "Red Guards" represent the only full incarnation of the proletarian spirit.

As of now, there seems little reason to believe that the conflicts occasioned by the "Cultural Revolution" have been resolved, nor is it by any means clear what its ultimate implications may be in the economic sphere. There are those who feel that Mao is once more preoccupied with mobilizing the people to "get the economy moving." But while there is no doubt that Mao ardently desires rapid economic development, I would suggest that even he learned in the course of 1958 that it is no easy matter to translate "Mao's Thought" into immediate economic results. It is thus not unlikely that his main immediate concern is not primarily with the economy, but rather with the saturation of his people's minds with his own vision of the good society, even if this does not lead to spectacular, immediate economic results. One need not expect Russian-type "Libermanism" in China, but neither is it yet clear that "Mao's Thought" must lead to a "Great Leap" type of economic experimentation in the immediate future, although there are now more and more indications that the leader wants to carry the activities of the "Red Guards" into the countryside and factories.

In the sphere of world politics, Mao's vision, in spite of its "radical nature," does not involve a more aggressive military posture. The world, to be sure, has not yet conformed to the Maoist projection, but the Yellow River has many bends. In the end, the Maoist model of revolution and of the good society will prove infectious in an unstable Third World. Meanwhile, China must offer this world a model of the good society, clearly marked off from that of the corrupt West.

Will Mao's ideas ultimately prevail? It seems to me that his terribly simple and constricted view of the human situation will prove as inapplicable to the human reality of China as to that of any other society, and that the forces resistant to his more extravagant dreams (forces which may represent a wide diversity of outlooks) will in the end prevail. Mao may not be totally deluded in believing that a society with a vast peasant population and many of its own cultural propensities will have to find its own path into the future. The China of the future may be radically different from the United States and the Soviet Union. But neither is it very likely to resemble Mao's utopia.

10

THE MAOIST IMAGE OF WORLD ORDER
(1967)

Are "The Chinese" prepared to accept the nation-state system that governs the international life of the West or are their images of the world and of China's place in it still governed by cultural habits derived from the remote past? It will be noted that this statement of alternatives leaves completely out of account a third category that dominates the discourse of the present Chinese Communist leadership itself—Marxism-Leninism and the "Thought of Mao Tse-tung." The latter is explicitly presented as marking a decisive break with both the culture of the past and the arrangements that govern the world of "capitalism and revisionism." Mao Tse-tung's present response to the above question no doubt would be a resounding rejection of both alternatives. We have, however, been educated by the profundities of the social sciences and depth psychology to discount conscious verbal behavior (at least on the part of others) in favor of larger "underlying" impersonal and

NOTE: This essay was first published in the *Journal of International Affairs*, vol. 21, no. 1 (1967).

unconscious forces. Nevertheless, in the following discussion the evolution of Communism in China will be treated as a third independent variable on the perhaps naive assumption that what people say must be considered as at least one factor in explaining their behavior.

In dealing with non-Western societies we easily slip into the vulgar cultural anthropological mode. The notion that there is one easily defined and unchanging Chinese image of world order and that any given Chinese will embody this image is not likely to meet much resistance on the part of a Western audience. Just as any given Navaho chief is presumed to be a typical case of the unchanging patterns of Navaho culture, so Mao Tse-tung may be thought of as the incarnation of a uniform Chinese cultural response. In dealing with this question we have chosen to focus our attention on Mao Tse-tung not merely because he has obviously played a decisive role in recent Chinese history, but precisely in order to underline the fact that he is not the incarnation of a "Chinese image of world order" but one complex individual whose responses to many of the situations he has confronted have been signally different from those of other Chinese. As of this writing, we are indeed acutely aware that Mao's perceptions of many matters may differ most markedly even from those of some of his closest associates in the Chinese Communist leadership. Furthermore his life, like that of many of his contemporaries, illustrates not cultural stasis but the enormous cultural crisis that China has experienced in the twentieth century.

Traditional Chinese Image of World Order. Before dealing with Mao Tse-tung we must say something about the "traditional" Chinese image of world order. It must be stated candidly that those now making a serious effort to understand the history of Chinese culture tend to be profoundly uneasy about the simple and static generalizations which

229

find such ready acceptance in these matters. In the West every generalization that we hazard about our international order must run the gauntlet of historians, specialists in international law, political theorists, and others, whereas generalizations about the millennial history of China still resound grandly in the vast cavern of our comparative ignorance. As our study of the Chinese past deepens, we will no doubt find that all of our present descriptions of the traditional order will undergo more and more qualification. Nevertheless, an attempt must be made.

In trying to discover the persistent features of the traditional image of world order, we find, first of all, the Chinese culture-area (*tien hsia*) conceived of as the center of a higher civilization that is ideally associated with a universal state governed by a universal king occupying a unique cosmic status. All surrounding states and principalities are ideally parts of this universal order and hierarchically subordinate to it in terms of tribute relationship. Of course such claims are not unique to China; they were made in ancient Mesopotamia, in Egypt, and in the Persian and Roman Empires. The uniqueness of the Chinese case lies in the persistence of such claims into the twentieth century. The Chinese universal kingship does not disappear from the scene until 1911.

The uniqueness of the Chinese experience does not necessarily spring from a particular cultural arrogance. It was in part due to certain contingent, external circumstances of Chinese history. In the ancient Middle East the absolute claims of Mesopotamian and Egyptian culture and universal kingship soon confronted each other. This fact may not have shaken Egyptian or Mesopotamian cultural confidence, but must certainly have done something to diminish the aura of these cultural and political claims among the various peoples who lived in surrounding and peripheral areas. China, on the other hand, remained unchallenged in its immediate vicinity by any polity whose cultural claims it felt obliged to consider. The only possible exception to this generalization is provided by Indian Buddhism. On the whole, however, Buddhism did not become the bearer of Indian political claims nor did it seriously challenge the basis of the Chinese universal kingship. The Chinese were not only unchallenged, they were also conscious of the influence of their own culture on surrounding peoples such as the Japanese, Vietnamese, and Koreans. And, as we know, "barbarian" rulers of China did tend in the long run to accept the absolute claims of the Chinese universal kingship. Thus experience tended to reinforce their claims.

One may, of course, raise questions about the degree to which the surrounding peoples accepted their assigned roles in the Chinese world order. The Japanese accepted cultural influence but managed to evade Chinese political claims. The Central Asian nomads and the peoples of Turkestan and Tibet probably never really accepted Chinese claims even where they were forced to assume the role of tribute bearers. Furthermore, there have been cases in the long history of China when emperors and officials have found it expedient to mute their own claims of political ascendancy. Still, if one considers the history of China in the last millennium in its broad sweep, it can be stated that the Chinese image of world order remained fundamentally intact.

It nevertheless may be asked how much this traditional Chinese image of the world order explains about the history of the foreign relations of the Chinese Empire. Does it, for instance, throw light on the question of Chinese aggressiveness? Actually, it was compatible with an extraordinarily wide range of attitudes and practices in the field of foreign policy. Surveying the long history of China one must arrive at the rather banal conclusion that it was compatible with both pacifistic isolationist policies and with aggressive expansionist policies. Even the attitude toward "barbarians" could run the gamut from the idealistic Mencian view that barbarians could be easily "civilized" by moral influence to the view that most of them were little better than beasts who could only be restrained by force. If Mao Tse-tung does indeed view the world through the eyes of his imperial predecessors, this throws little light on the future course of his policies. One would have to know which predecessors provide his model.

The traditional image probably had its most fateful effect on Chinese behavior during the nineteenth century, when it prevented an adjustment to the remorseless assault of the Western international system. The Chinese ruling class confronted a West as firmly committed to the universal validity of its conception of absolute nation-state sovereignty as the Chinese Empire was to its own view. Indeed, this conception had been given added weight by the rise of nineteenth-century nationalism. The history of China during the last half of the nineteenth century was marked by what Western observers regarded as an obscurantist, obdurate, and at times comical effort to resist the normal patterns of international relations. In retrospect it appears that the imperial court's resistance was probably based on an obscure yet sound instinct. The Chinese monarchy was, after all, inextricably tied to a cosmology of universal kingship. Whether it could have survived the crumbling of this cosmology and been converted into a Western-style "national" monarchy remains a moot point.

Chinese Nationalism and the Western Image. Despite this resistance, however, the striking fact remains that by the turn of the century many articulate Chinese had made the qualitative leap. They had come to accept the Western system with all its conventions and were prepared to think of China as one nation-state among others. Figures such as Yen Fu and Liang Chi-ch'ao, whose writings were to exercise an enormous influence on the generation of Chinese now in its seventies, were entirely prepared to jettison the traditional conception of China's place in the world as the price of China's survival as a political entity. They had not renounced China's greatness but were prepared to rethink it in terms of modern nationalism. This was true not only of nationalist revolutionaries such as Sun Yat-sen, but even of many of the intellectual leaders of the monarchist movement who had given up the commitment to universal kingship in favor of something like a national monarchy. For at least a small but decisive segment of China's population, the bases of the traditional conception of China's place in the world had decisively collapsed. Again, however, we must rid ourselves of the tyranny of cultural holism. This collapse did not necessarily involve a total break with the whole range of habits of thought and behavior inherited from the past. It was entirely possibe for the same individual to accept the concept of China as a nation-state among others without abandoning other traditions. It was simply that this particular sector of the cultural heritage had proven itself peculiarly vulnerable to the assault of new experience. Traditionalists as well as Westernizers were committed to the survival of China as a political entity and were by now aware that its survival depended on the acceptance of the game as it was played in the West.

To be sure, even after the arrival of modern nationalism one can find a tendency among some Chinese intellectuals and politicians to speak of China's universal cultural contribution to mankind. Sun Yat-sen, a man without deep roots in the cultural heritage, became more and more insistent in his later years on China's universal mission and the contributions of Chinese civilization to mankind. Is such thinking to be regarded as a reversion to the sinocentrism of the past or can it be explained as analogous to similar phenomena elsewhere? Nationalism everywhere displays a tendency to universalize the particular. The German will insist on the universal superiority of *Deutsche Kultur,* the French on their *"mission civilisatrice,"* and the Americans on the "American way of life." It used to be common to explain the transnational element in Soviet Communism in terms of Holy Russia's messianism and the doctrine of the third Rome. Admittedly, we are here in an area where the boundaries between all our well-defined categories become hazy. The only tangible method of dealing with this question, crude as it may be, is to ask whether the Chinese are prepared to play the game (loose and ambiguous as its rules are) in terms of the prevailing international system.

Chiang Kai-shek provides us with a good test case. Ever since the 1930's he has been much more insistent than Sun on the superiority of Chinese traditional values and their applicability to the problems of modern society. Whether this commitment is authentic or simply a manifestation of national pride—or both—I shall not presume to judge. Yet there is no evidence whatsoever that he has not accepted the nation-state system or not operated within its framework. His famous manifesto on "China's Destiny" (written under his imprimatur) is at once profoundly "traditionalistic" in tone and deep, even orthodox in its commitment to the principles of national sovereignty as defined in the West. In his conception of world order, he owes infinitely more to Bodin than to Confucius.

Turning to the biography of Mao Tse-tung, one can make a good case for the assertion that he has lived his life within a basically Chinese context, particularly if we hasten to add that the word "Chinese" refers not only to a changeless cultural heritage but to a twentieth-century China in crisis. The sensitive years of early childhood were spent in a rural society untouched by any direct Western influence, and his earliest view of the world was derived from Chinese sources. Again, it is important to note that these sources were by no means as homogeneous in their message as Westerners might think. The message he derived from his beloved Chinese epic novels was not precisely the same as that of the Four Books. One could even find in the heritage inspiration for rebelliousness. It will not do to speak of the traditional elements in Mao without attempting to define what these elements are. In spite of this "rootedness" in China, there is no reason to think that during his formative years of intellectual growth after 1910 Mao did not come to accept without reservation the Western image of world order. His knowledge of the world at large was wholly derived from the writings of Yen Fu, Liang Chi-ch'ao, and translations of Western writings, all of which simply assumed the premises of the nation-state system. The young pre-Communist Mao can be called a modern nationalist without the slightest reservation. Like many of his contemporaries he dreamt of China's resurgence, but of its resurgence as a great power in a world of great powers.

The Communist Dimension. Mao Tse-tung was to be converted to Marxism-Leninism, however, and with Marxism-Leninism we confront a new and complicating dimension. The October Revolution, as we know, was designed to shatter the whole "bourgeois" nation-state structure. Marx belonged to a whole group of nineteenth-century thinkers who regarded the international system of their time as anachronistic and moribund, and while we are all aware of the transformations that Marxism experienced at the hands of Lenin, there is every reason to believe that Lenin genuinely shared Marx's transnational outlook. In this he reflected the cosmopolitanism of a large sector of the Russian radical intelligentsia, which was quite unable to identify with the national glory of the Tsarist state. Lenin genuinely expected the October Revolution to serve as the spark for a world revolution that would dissolve the whole rotten international structure.

It is true that as a practical politician Lenin had devoted more attention to the "national question" than anyone else in the Marxist movement. He had created doctrinal rationalizations for harnessing resentful "bourgeois nationalism" to the wagon of revolution, and he had a genuine insight into the future role of such resentful nationalism in Asia. Lenin approached "bourgeois nationalism" from the outside as a cold manipulator, yet many of the formulae of Marxism-Leninism as they existed at the time of Lenin's death were already available for nationalist purposes. As a matter of fact, many of the young Chinese who were attracted to Marxism-Leninism in the early twenties (Mao among them) were already Chinese nationalists and as such were particularly attracted by those aspects of the Leninist theory of imperialism that seemed to explain China's national humiliation. This does not mean that they were completely insensitive to the apocalyptic cosmopolitan message of Communism. Indeed, some converts to Communism in China belonged to that small company of Chinese intellectuals who were ready to leap from the universalism of the older Chinese system to the transnational universalism of the new cosmopolitan philosophies from the West. The young Mao did not, on the whole, belong to their company. Surveying the evolution of his thought from 1921 to the present, one feels that Communism did not displace his nationalism but rather supplemented and complicated it.

In dealing with the relationship between "world Communism" and nationalism, we must first of all realize that we are not dealing with abstract essences but with a dynamic, evolving drama that has still not ended. It is a drama, moreover, in which the Chinese Communists themselves have played a large and ambiguous role.

In accepting Soviet Communism the Chinese Communists, including Mao, had of course accepted the notion of a supreme source of spiritual and political authority lying outside of China—this despite their nationalist passions. Furthermore, when this authority became completely tied to the interests of one territorial state—the Soviet Union—most of them continued to accept this authority. Only a handful of Chinese Trotskyists rejected the theory of "socialism in one country," and the supremacy of Moscow's authority in the Communist world continued to be accepted in Mao's China until the very end of the 1950's.

All of this has led some to suggest that the Chinese Communists, including Mao, in accepting the hierarchic superiority of the Soviet Union were in effect reverting to the hierarchic-vertical mode of thinking so characteristic of the traditional order and rejecting the unfamiliar Western notion of equally sovereign states. I find this notion difficult to accept. It is first of all quite clear, as we have noted, that the Western conception *had* been accepted without difficulty by many of the future members of the Communist Party. One of the main attractions of the Marxist-Leninist doctrine was that it provided a devastating critique of the arrogant imperialist West from a "modern" Western point of view. It provided an excellent way of dealing with the dilemma to which Mao referred retrospectively in his speech on "The People's Democratic Dictatorship" in 1949, namely, that "the teachers [the West] are constantly attacking their pupils." The young people who joined the party were probably much more conscious of the weapons it provided against Western *hubris* than of its implied subordination to Moscow.

There were, of course, other reasons why the formulae of Marxism-Leninism proved attractive. Its assumption of knowledge regarding the direction of history, its promise of a total solution of China's immense problems of poverty,

237

corruption, and disorganization must all be given great weight. I doubt very much that the attractions of the hierarchic concept of world order played a very significant role. It was, after all, a hierarchic order that placed the Chinese not at the summit but in an inferior position. The traditional order was based not on a mere abstract notion that there ought to be a hierarchic order in the relations of peoples, but on the rather specific complacent belief that China ought to be at the summit of this hierarchy. It would perhaps be more accurate to say that the Chinese Communists accepted Moscow's authority not because of the hierarchic implications of Soviet Communism but in spite of them. Their faith in certain basic assumptions of Marxism-Leninism was sufficiently strong to override their nationalist resistance.

This is particularly true, it seems to me, of Mao Tse-tung. He had accepted from Marxism-Leninism, as he understood it, many of the categories in terms of which the world is described; and many of these categories have continued to govern his image of the world to this very day. Until very recently this acceptance also involved a genuine acknowledgment of Moscow's ideological authority and of the Soviet Union as a model of socialism. It is precisely in this area, it seems to me, that a tension has existed from the very outset between the nationalist and transnationalist elements in his outlook.

We know of course that once he achieved ascendancy within the Chinese Communist movement during the Yenan period, he began to project his image of himself as the man who was applying the universal truths of Marxism-Leninism to the particularities of the Chinese situation. And he was doing this at a time when the doctrine was still dominant in Moscow that the authority to apply Marxist-Leninist doctrine to particular national situations was

238

the exclusive prerogative of the Kremlin. We know that the nationalist coloration of Chinese Communism intensified during this period. In retrospect it does not seem at all plausible to assume that Mao Tse-tung was simply an "international Communist" manipulating Chinese nationalism from the outside. What is more probable is that he assumed that the aspirations of Chinese nationalism and of world Communism could be easily reconciled. He may have genuinely believed—even after 1949—that, whatever the difficulties, a Chinese Communist state would be able to maintain general harmony with the Soviet Union in terms of certain overriding shared beliefs, without renouncing any of its basic sovereign prerogatives as a nation-state. After Stalin's death, we know that the Chinese Communist government did everything possible to encourage those tendencies in Moscow that favored greater national autonomy within the world Communist movement; and since the outbreak of the Sino-Soviet conflict, the Chinese have, on one side of their polemic, made themselves the spokesmen of the most orthodox doctrine of national sovereignty within the Communist world. It is the Chinese who have promulgated one of the most striking doctrines in the whole church history of Communism, namely, that the decisions of any given national party (including the CPSU) are binding only within the area under the jurisdiction of that party.

All of this, of course, is highly "dialectic" in intention. One insists on the national sovereignty of states within the Soviet orbit in order to undermine the authority of the Soviet Union. Presumably, in a future international Communist order centered in Peking there will no longer be such insistence on national sovereignty. The fact remains that the Chinese Communist movement has itself played a crucial role in the unfolding relationship of Communism to nationalism. Whatever Mao's subjective intentions may be, Chinese Communism has helped to bring about what seems to be the triumph of the nation-state system over the transnational claims of Marxism-Leninism.

To be sure, in Peking the transnational aspirations now seem more alive than ever. The center of Communist authority, in Mao's view, has now definitely shifted from Moscow to Peking. True Marxism-Leninism is now dispensed only from Peking. It is thus precisely since the Moscow-Peking rift that those who emphasize the traditional cultural bases of Mao's image of the world have felt their case vindicated. Once again the Middle Kingdom has become the center of the "Way," and like the emperors of old, Mao Tse-tung is the highest source of both political authority and spiritual truth.

It is very difficult either to prove or to disprove a proposition of this nature. I have tried to demonstrate that both China and Mao Tse-tung have gone through a most tortuous course during the period between the collapse of the older world order and the present state of affairs, and that during that period many Chinese (including Mao at one stage in his life) had come to accept the nation-state framework without any difficulty, whatever their relationship may have been to other aspects of the traditional culture. The cosmology on the basis of which Mao asserts his authority is not the cosmology that underlay the traditional kingship. It is a cosmology that includes constant appeals to the authority of two "barbarians" named Marx and Lenin. It is of course true that the "Thought of Mao Tse-tung" is acquiring more and more weight within the ideological framework. Yet in appealing for support abroad the Chinese continue to emphasize the purity of their Marxism-Leninism. It may well be that this latest development in Chinese Communism resonates as it were with certain aspects of the traditional image of world order; however, the crucial question here is not whether it resonates with the traditional image but whether it is determined by it. If China's international behavior is determined by cultural images that have their roots in prehistory, we need not expect any speedy adjustments to a world that does not fit this image. If it is shaped by the more recent history of China and by a doctrine that is itself in a state of crisis and flux, if it is even shaped by the personal vision of Mao Tse-tung, who can in no way be equated with China, we must be alert to the possibility of sweeping shifts in the future.

Even as of this writing—in the very throes of the "Cultural Revolution"—China's relations with the world operate on two levels. On one level we find Mao's "higher" vision, in which China will be the center of a resurgent, purified Communist world. On another level we find the Chinese carrying on conventional diplomatic and commercial relations within the accepted nation-state framework, and even pressing the principle of national sovereignty within the Communist world. The aging Mao, to be sure, is deeply committed to his grand transnational vision and seems quite willing to sacrifice the possibility of more conventional diplomatic successes to the achievement of that vision.

These hopes for the realization of the vision, however, are not based on a programmatic blueprint but on certain expectations regarding the future course of world history. If these hopes are not realized in the foreseeable future, if the nation-state system proves as recalcitrant to the transnational hopes of Mao Tse-tung as it has to the hopes of others, will China be able to adjust to the world as it is? We have argued here that China has, since the beginning of the twentieth century, already demonstrated its ability to adjust to this system and that the process of adjustment has continued even under the Communists. Paradoxically, Mao Tse-tung has himself played a fateful role in weaken-

241

ing transnational authority within the Communist world. He has failed to consider the possibility that in undermining the supreme authority of Moscow in the Communist world he may have simply undermined the very notion of such authority in that world. Finally, there is now more room than ever for doubting whether all of Mao's colleagues within the Communist movement share the full ardor of his transnational vision.

I do not mean to suggest that the Western international system is more deeply rooted in some eternal, metahistorical order of things than the traditional Chinese conception of world order. In a world where China must continue to confront two other formidable world powers; in a world where there is an overriding passion for local and regional political independence; and in a world where none of the prevailing transnational ideologies, religions, or cultures have been able to establish their universal claims, the present international system will continue to provide a more acceptable framework of world order than anything else in sight, for the Chinese as well as for the rest of us.

Index

INDEX

Africa, 24, 25, 36, 139, 154, 155, 157, 158, 160, 186, 188, 189, 190, 197

Agrarian society, 133, 134, 193

"Agriculture as the base," 171, 182, 210

Albania, 45, 90, 91

Algeria, 157, 160, 191

American: "exceptionalism," 52; imperialism, 28; policy, 128, 192, 201; "policies and Chinese Visions," 186; social science, 7; Soviet nuclear monopoly, 212; views on new generation in China, 225

Anti-Leninism, 147

Apparatchiki, 68, 76

Army: ideological remolding of, 166; and Maoist line, 221; as model for Chinese society, 213; and party, 206, 221; People's Liberation, 20, 42, 184, 214, 223, 226; professionalization of, 170, 183, 212; and "Red Guards," 226; revolutionary, 154; Soviet 217

Art, 104, 115

Asia, 24, 25, 36, 57, 64, 65, 76, 77, 85, 89, 112, 116, 139, 154, 155, 188, 189, 190, 204, 236; Central, 231; East, 130, 157, 158; Southeast, 194, 202

Authority: coercive, 143; of CPSU, 141; in Communist world, 17, 26, 32, 33, 38, 146, 187, 197, 237,

Authority (*cont.*)
241; in cultural sphere, 115; Moscow's, 141, 143, 144, 197, 237, 238, 242; and myth of Communist Party, 140; and paths to socialism, 139; and Sino-Soviet relations, 130–148, 238; Stalin's, 74, 141, 142; ultimate instance of, 145, 197, 198

Bandung: Chou En-lai and, 188; doctrine, 135, 189; line, 154, 155, 156, 157, 188, 202

Belgrade, 37, 93, 94

Bethune, Norman, 214

Bloc, Communist: China and, 117–129; China as partner in, 123; and Chinese domestic affairs, 119; and confrontation with "imperialism," 210; and death of Stalin, 181; and "Hundred Flowers" campaign, 120; and Moscow's authority, 136, 143, 145; orthodoxy in, 125, 128; solidarity of, 33, 34, 210

Bodin, Jean, 234

"Bourgeois democratic": measures, 51; tasks, 56, 85; stage, 83; demands, 84; period, 114

Bourgeoisie: current Chinese use of as term, 41, 42; elimination of, 60, 84; education of, 60; Kuusinen on, 18; leadership of bourgeois revolution by, 70; monopolistic, 49; national, 59,

245